D0720288

A Wise Dog Named Jake

Lessons on life, survival, tolerance, and
love from an extraordinary stray dog

Brigitte Finkiewicz

Copyright © 2018 Brigitte Finkiewicz

The right of Brigitte Finkiewicz to be identified as the Author of the Work
has been asserted by her in accordance with the Copyright, Designs and
Patents Act 1988

ISBN-10: 1983808997
ISBN-13: 978-1983808999

Dedication

To anyone who has lost a parent, a friend, a pet...
And to my father for the legacy he left me.

CONTENTS

ACKNOWLEDGMENTS

I would like to thank first and foremost, my partner and significant other, David Osborn. You read each phase of this book, and your positive feedbacks gave me the incentive to continue my task. Your input in helping me design the cover of this book was paramount.

I would like to also acknowledge and thank my friend and fellow volunteer Suzanne Marion, for taking the time to sit down with me and review the text and content of this book.

Thank you to my friend Sondra Simon for your enthusiasm and support.

Last, I have to thank the extraordinary dog who came into my life in 1985. Jake, you made my life richer....

Brigitte Finkiewicz

Chapter 1

Getting to Know Each Other

The street to our apartment complex was quiet. I pulled into my parking spot and turned off the engine, my head still buzzing with the events of the day. A few weeks earlier, I had started an engineering job, and it was nerve-racking to learn new standards and work myself into the new team. When I stepped out of the car, I took a deep breath and smiled in anticipation of a well-deserved quiet evening. It was a warm night as we often have in June in Texas; the moon was illuminating the water in the pool near the upstairs apartment we occupied.

When I approached our building, I looked up and noticed that Allan was on the porch, bent over the picnic table, busy with something underneath him. Wondering what he was up to, I rushed upstairs and found myself facing a large dog. His round brown eyes were staring at me, his tail was wagging slowly, his skinny back legs were barely supporting his weight, but his head was held high with a sort of pride and serenity. He was black and brown, with floppy ears, and had the head and markings of a German shepherd. I stood on the stairs, looking at him and wondering how much stress I could take for one day.

The dog was quietly studying me, pointing his nose in my direction, absorbing my scent. A wave of peaceful bliss surrounded me and without a thought I walked up to him and hugged him. He greeted me as if he had always known me, with a quiet assertive demeanor and at that moment, when my eyes met his, and my fingers touched his neck and powerful chest, I knew that he would be my dog. I named him Jake.

He had walked by the pool area, looking for food when Allan noticed him. It did not take much persuading for Jake to walk upstairs. He looked hungry and his body was covered with wounds, some still spewing pus. His ribs were showing, and his hind leg muscles were very thin and weak. His body was literally eating into itself to survive. I knew the quiet anticipated evening was not going to happen. We did not have any dog food, so a trip to the store was necessary. I sent Allan to pick up a small bag, because until I researched what the best food would be for our new friend, the cheap brand would have to do for now.

Alone with Jake, I decided to clean his wounds, so I asked him to follow me to the spare bathroom, where I filled the tub with warm water. "Get in," I said, pointing to the tub. He looked at me, turned to the tub and slowly lifted a paw over the edge and entered the tub without a fuss. I was flabbergasted, because I had not believed when I gave my command that he would obey. I stood there, wide eyed and open mouthed for a second while he patiently and calmly waited for me. When I got my wits back, I kneeled in front of the tub, grabbed the shampoo, and gently massaged his ravaged body.

I could feel every rib. I followed the curve of his

belly; it was like a big cavity, a skin holding a protruding ribcage with nothing inside. "Where have you been? How long have you been living on the street, my poor Jake?" I asked him, my heart already filled with love. His eyes were looking into mine, like he had surrendered to me his whole soul. It took a few months of healthy food and tender care to see the beautiful dog emerge from this pitiful carcass.

From the get-go, I realized that Jake was a very special dog. He would observe me with his piercing eyes, and at times, I would swear he was reading my mind. If I was getting ready for work, he would just lie in his bed, following my every move, as if he wanted to enjoy my company until the very last moment. If I intended to take him on a walk, before I had even grabbed the leash, he would wait by the door, sitting straight, his tail sweeping the floor with a slow wag.

Jake learned all the basic commands in a few days. He would walk by my side sometimes off leash, always keeping me in sight and responding immediately to any change in direction. I worked long hours too far from home to come back at lunch time, and he would stay inside for as many as twelve hours without any accident. Of course, the second I would open the door in the evening all bets were off, and I had to follow him, as his bladder dripped steadily all the way to the bottom of the stairs, where he finally would relieve himself in the nearby bushes for what seemed to be fifteen minutes nonstop.

It was 1985, and despite my youthful age and my addiction to aerobic dance, I had chronic back pain, which prevented me at times from walking up and down the stairs. Allan worked offshore sometimes three weeks at a time, so Jake and I spent a lot of time together. On the days that my back was hurting too much to take him out for a walk, he would go downstairs on his own, do his business, and come back immediately to stay by my side. Jake was shy about relieving himself in public, so he would back up into the bushes, where no one could see him, and I was thankful for this amusing behavior on the days I was not able to pick up his waste.

Many tenants who lived in the area knew Jake; he would always get a lot of attention from everyone. The pool area, which was off limits to pets, was available to Jake, and even though the rental office was nearby, they did not seem to mind the big black dog sitting by my side when I was lounging in the sun or having a late evening with friends. Jake was always a part of the festivities in the club house as well. Allan and I hosted several of our holidays, for many of our friends, who like us had no family in Texas. Everyone loved Jake, and Jake loved everyone.

Even our neighbor's big cat seemed to tolerate Jake's presence. Blue, a very large brown-and-white Siamese cat, perched on our neighbor's porch every day, would scrutinize everyone who walked by. He tolerated people, but no cat or dog was welcome in the pool area. Blue would chase the terrified animal, who would run desperately away from the attack. However, Jake seemed to have a free pass, and they lived in harmony next to each other. At times Blue would stare at Jake, from the top of his throne, almost daring him to make a move, but Jake would just walk steadily, without a look, and his calm demeanor would let Blue know that he respected him and there was no reason for a fight.

The first veterinarian who treated Jake when we found him (or when he found us) said that most of the wounds on his body appeared to be dog bites. Jake was a survivor, and even a cat as dominant as Blue was not about to impact his resilience or change his calm, and loving personality. We always wondered if he had escaped a dog fighting ring, where he might have been used as a bait for prize dogs.

Dogfighting is a felony in Texas, but many sophisticated operations were at the time suspected in Montgomery, Harris and Tyler Counties near Houston. In these operations, only spectators known personally to the group could attend the bloody battles. High-stakes bets were placed weeks before a fight, with participants calling for a dog of specific weight and gender and dictating how many weeks the animal should be trained. Bets placed on one dog could reach $80,000 or more, so when training these dogs, owners used smaller, weaker dogs, called "bait dogs," to prevent injury on their prize animals. Most of the time, the bait dog was killed or left to die in a field or discarded like a bag of garbage on a side road.

There is an area in Houston known as the "Corridor of Cruelty," where fighting dog ring's victims are dumped, as well as unwanted pets. The corridor is an area more than a mile wide, located in northeast Houston near the Little York exit off the Eastex Freeway. In 2010, CNN ran a story about a woman named Deborah Hoffman, who started a nonprofit named Corridor Rescue. She started rescuing these dogs and shed the light on the neglect and abuse they endure.

Since then, numerous criminal cases have been filed against people who have dumped their dogs. Not only did Hoffman bring the problem to the attention of the police department, who installed cameras along the corridor, and the district attorney, who got involved, but she also rehomed many of the dogs that could be saved. She was quoted in the CNN interview as saying, "One of the saddest cases is when I come across one (dog), in a large green Hefty trash bag. Some of the dogs that we find in bags have serious wounds, most likely from dog fighting".

She came across the corridor in 2006 while volunteering for a rescue group, and in 2008 a return visit moved her to rally her community for help. She said, "I took my twelve-year-old daughter with me, and we spent the afternoon driving this neighborhood. We both were literally in tears by the end of the journey". Soon after, those tears turned into action. Her group is still rescuing dogs today. (www.corridorrescue.org).

It was apparent by the scars Jake wore on his body that he had been in many dog fights, and most likely mistreated by people around him. Despite his bad experiences, he did not hate or fear man or beast.

Jake was strong and inspiring, and I often asked myself how he had truly survived without being tainted. So many of us become contaminated by traumatic events and we go through life holding back our true potential for joy, love, and creativity, because of the fear or pain experienced in the past or present. Jake had channeled his energy forward instead of letting the past hinder him.

It was infectious to see him grow into a beautiful, healthy, and self-assured dog and it pushed me to stare at my own shortcomings. The most debilitating aspect of my life was related to my back problem. I basically was relying on daily chiropractic adjustments, which helped for about one hour, then the spasms would take over my lower back again, and I would suffer at the office and all the way home, until I could finally lie down.

I decided to be pro-active and look for other solutions. I adopted a positive attitude, built hope of healing, researched medical papers, and attended seminars and back anatomy classes, and one day I stumbled upon the McKenzie Method. The book *Treat Your Own Back* by Robin McKenzie was the validation of my own thinking. In chapter 1, the author writes, "The main point of this book is that the management of your back is your responsibility." The words, "your responsibility" were written in bold letters. I wanted to be in charge of my own body, and this author was giving me the tools to achieve my quest in living a more independent healthy life.

The advice from the book touched upon every aspect of one's daily activities, the way we sit, walk, and do physical work. I followed every exercise and piece of advice each hour of my day, and soon I noticed the gradual improvement in my back. I cancelled my chiropractic appointment and never went back. I took charge of my own healing, and each day, Jake would lie beside me, clear reminder of what resilience is, while I stretched and strengthened my back and stomach muscles. I competed against my own handicap to win control of my life. It was invigorating to realize the strength within me and the possibilities. Jake had opened a new horizon for me and I felt free!

Changing the course of my life because of a dog was not a foreign idea to me. I remember during my childhood the paralyzing fear that would overcome me if someone with a dog would share the same walkway. My mother would have to hold my hand tightly while I struggled to get away. We never learned why I was so afraid of dogs; I was barely four years old, and my mom could not recall any bad encounter.

One day in the south of France where we were vacationing, I accompanied my mother and sister to the boulangerie to pick up some fresh croissants and a baguette. The boulangerie owner told us that her cocker spaniel had just given birth to a litter of puppies, and she asked if we wanted to see them. My sister was excited about it, but I stayed quiet, holding on to my mother's dress.

In the back room, in a basket filled with warm blankets, the young mama dog was lying calmly with her four puppies. I was intrigued by the little brown fuzzy animals. I was observing the scene at a safe distance, when the lady turned to me and said, "Veus-tu caresser les petits chiots?" (Do you want to touch the little puppies?) I wanted to touch them, but I was afraid of the mother dog, so still holding on to my mother's dress, I signaled negatively with my head.

A Wise Dog Named Jake

After an exchange with my mother, the lady insisted and took my little hand, while speaking to me very calmly, to bring me close to the basket.

I wanted to resist and maybe even throw a tantrum to get away, but it was not in my makeup to express myself in such fashion. In those days children were told to trust adults and go along with them. With the emotion flowing into my four-year-old heart, I did not notice the mama dog lifting her head and gently licking the top of my hand. When I realized what had just happened, I was stunned, and I stayed near the basket, wide eyed, a smile slowly drawing on my lips.

I was enjoying the gentle affection the dog was demonstrating toward me. My heart was not pounding; the debilitating fear I had felt before about all dogs had disappeared. I suddenly felt at home stroking the babies' soft fur, while the sweet cocker spaniel looked upon me. She had reached deep inside me to ease my fear, which no one had been capable of doing, and she had soothed my emotions to empower me and open a new path.

This was the beginning of my love and respect for all animals. In our early teens, my sister and I rescued and nursed back to health several birds found in the street. We even picked up a small lost dog, who later was reunited with his owner. Little did I know that the mama dog had opened the path my life would take for years to come.

Jake staring at me and watching my every move. Allan had built a bed for him, and it was very clear that he enjoyed having his own domain.

Jake attending the festivities at the club house. He enjoyed the attention he was getting and the cameras flashing all around him.

Brigitte Finkiewicz

Jake attended many parties and was not shy about wearing costumes during the whole time we entertained. This picture was taken during a costume party where Jake was dressed as his name-sake: Jake from *The Blues Brothers*.

A Wise Dog Named Jake

Jake and I had settled into a pleasant routine; we had made many friends around the apartment complex, where we spent most of our time waiting for Allan's return from offshore. Of course, there was always the occasional tenant whose dog was not so friendly. Close to the laundry room resided such a person, who did not have the sense to keep her pet inside or under control.

One Saturday morning, Jake and I were heading out to the laundry room. My clothes basket was particularly full that day, and I could hardly see where I was placing my feet as we were walking along the narrow path. When we passed an opened door, I barely saw the shadow running toward me but his bark startled me and it all happened so fast, I did not have time to react. Fortunately, Jake sprang into action immediately. With a ferocious growl, he threw his large chest against the barking dog, and after a tumble, the chase was on. They disappeared behind the buildings; I could still hear the dog barking as he was running away from Jake.

I am not sure what happened to the dog; no one mentioned his aggressive behavior after that incident, despite the many complaints that were made against his owner earlier that year. I am sure Jake did not hurt him; he was too kind, but he had come to my rescue on that day, and I was very thankful he was taking his job as my protector very seriously. However, his job was just starting, and our life together would prove to be, should I say, rather interesting...

Later that year, Allan got a short contract assignment in New York state to bring equipment to a job site. The company truck, full of heavy machinery in the bed, was very spacious inside, and Allan wanted Jake and me to accompany him on the long trip. We decided to make it a small vacation and packed up for a two-week getaway. We set up the back seat for Jake so that he would be comfortable during the long drive. We planned our trajectory with sight-seeing deviations for each state we would visit on the way and embarked on our adventure. Jake seemed to enjoy being with us, watching the cars and trucks go by. He would lie down on the bed we created for him on the back seat and never moved unless we stopped to let him out for a walk or to relieve himself.

Texas was almost behind us, and we had turned off the radio to listen to the CB radio. Amused by the truckers' chitchats, we decided to engage in the conversation to pass time. However, if you want to fit in, you should be aware of the CB terminology or trucker slang. A "bear" is a trooper or law enforcement officer. "Back door" means something behind you. "Bear bite" is a speeding ticket, a "bird dog" is a radar detector, and a "chicken coop" is a weigh station. "Come back" is an invitation for the other driver to talk, and a 4-wheeler is any passenger vehicle. Most truckers use a nickname, and I decided that mine would be "Joan of Arc" after a young French heroine who fought the British in the early 1420s. The name fitted me, because of my French accent that the truckers soon detected.

As we passed by a radar detector, I went on to say: "This is Joan of Arc, bird dog in my back door," and I continued by giving road names.

A Wise Dog Named Jake

"Come Back," I heard someone say. I repeated my information in the same fashion, trying to hide the big smile on my face and the giggle that was coming up. "Copy, Joan of Arc, this is Old Cowboy; how are you doing?".

"Hello, Old Cowboy, I am doing great," I answered with a giggle. Someone else joined our conversation, asking where I was and where I came from with "that accent"?

The road was full of Mack trucks, livestock haulers, and other large semi-trailers. The chitchat continued for a few miles as they tried to figure out what heavy truck I belonged to. They did not know we were in a passenger vehicle, just a work truck, so the conversation went on between them while they searched for the mysterious Joan of Arc.

Allan and I were laughing and enjoying ourselves when we attempted to pass a semitrailer and maintained speed with it for a brief moment. I looked up beside me at the driver; he looked right back at me with a large smile, and his horn sounded loud, like a triumphant salute! I waved and smiled at him, and the CB Radio exploded with exclamations, "I see Joan of Arc, she has a pretty smile."

Another trucker responded, "She is in a red 4-wheeler, I see her too." The horns were still sounding as we drove past a few large trucks, with drivers glued to their CB radios, waving at us.

As the night arrived the chatter on the CB radio quieted down, and we continued in silence on our journey to the motel. Jake had spent the entire day relaxing in the back seat, watching the countryside go by, and listening to our laughs. While Allan went to the motel front desk, I waited in the truck. Jake got up from his comfortable bed and with a slow wag signaled his contentment on having arrived at our destination. He stretched and looked around him, noticeably happy but still calm and quiet, a perfect example of a great traveler.

Keys in hand we drove to our unit and backed the truck into our space, facing the window of our bedroom. We hoped that no one would be able to steal the equipment without Jake or us waking up. Exhausted from our drive, we went to bed early that night, and within minutes, we fell into a much needed deep sleep.

Around 2:00 a.m., Jake started barking at the window, scratching the glass with his front paws and running frenetically from one side to the other behind the heavy curtains. When I woke up, my heart was pumping in my chest, and the rush of adrenaline made me suddenly hot and clammy. We jumped out of bed; it took us a few seconds to collect our thoughts, and by the time we turned on the light and looked out of the window, we heard the screeching of tires in the parking lot, and all became quiet again.

We slowly opened the door and eased ourselves quietly outside, looking around cautiously for anyone or any danger. The parking lot was quiet; the soft lights illuminating each unit threw suspicious shadows at every corner. We felt uneasy. The equipment and the truck seemed untouched, except for one strap that was dangling off the side of the truck. I turned to Jake, who was standing quietly by my side, and I threw my arms around his neck and softly whispered, "Thank you my boy."

We never could fall back to sleep that night and spent the rest of our early morning turning and tossing in bed, listening for every noise around us. However, the only sound filling our still dark bedroom was of Jake, snoring peacefully by my side of the bed. I was wondering if at some time in my life, I would ever be able, like Jake, to live for the moment and get back to peaceful harmony within seconds after the excitement had passed, despite how intense that moment was?

Brigitte Finkiewicz

Jake watching the road on our trip to NY state.

Chapter 2

The Big Move

Allan and I got married in 1986, and of course Jake was a part of the festivities. The seamstress I hired to make the bridesmaids' lavender dresses also made the matching bow ties for the males in the wedding party, including the white bow ties for the groom and Jake. Everyone looked so beautiful; my heart was dancing in my chest like a butterfly on a warm sunny day. Jake looked handsome in his white satin bow, and he was very popular with the bridesmaids. In the madness of all the activities he managed to remain calm. Before leaving my apartment for the ceremony, holding on to my father's arm, I looked back at Jake and took a deep breath, almost trying to inhale a part of his calm demeanor. I smiled at him with all the joy I had in my heart, and his tail thumped the floor in response. He knew this was a special moment.

My parents, who had made the long flight from France a week earlier to be with us, stayed with Jake and looked after him when we left for a short honeymoon. My dad particularly enjoyed Jake's company even though Jake kept on licking his toes for no apparent reason. We believe he did it because my dad's reaction was to laugh and interact with him, and Jake assumed it was a game. One rainy day during our absence, after waiting for the severe weather to move through, my dad decided that Jake probably had to relieve himself. He estimated that he had been inside for too long, and he felt sorry for "the poor dog." He put on Allan's raincoat, took one of my larger umbrellas, and set out to walk Jake despite the rain.

Mom told me that she waited for them for at least thirty minutes. By that time, the weather had turned worse, and a torrential rain was hitting the trees and bushes, the wind turning over the lawn chairs and tables by the pool area. My father was seventy-nine years old, and Jake could have easily pulled him to the ground, so she was starting to pace back and forth in front of the large bedroom window. The branches of the nearby trees were slapping the building and making her uneasy.

Her heart jumped in her chest when she saw the umbrella turned inside out; underneath it, my dad was hiding from the wind, head tucked into his chest, trying to keep the rain out of his eyes. Jake was trotting beside him as slow as my dad was able and willing to walk. The two of them were soaked and got vigorously toweled dry and reprimanded by my mom, but everyone was safe and sound. Jake had kept a steady slow walk despite the wind and rain so that my father could safely return home.

After this rainy day, I have thought many times of the tolerance and calm Jake exhibited to keep my father safe. It made me consider my own, sometimes impatient behavior. I was a young vibrant woman full of energy, and I had many times complained about my father's shopping habits, which included stopping and looking meticulously at every item we encountered. It was time for me to walk his speed even when the storm inside me was telling me to rush. It is not easy for a young twenty-nine-year-old to appreciate the pace and strategy of her parents' life.

The gap between our generations was enormous, but listening to the stories of my father's military service during World War II was the connection we had. I was thirsty for knowledge; history was my passion, and the tales of his many struggles and victories captivated me.

He had left the pogroms (the organized massacres against Jewish communities) and anti-Semitism of a prewar Poland for the stability and welcome of France. When Germany waged war on France, he had volunteered to fight and defend his adopted country. Like him, in my late teens I had left my home and country to seek the promised land. After several years of volunteering in my hometown Jewish community and being confronted by bigotry against Jews, I wanted to give a part of my life to the Jewish country of my ancestors. After almost four years in a kibbutz in the north of Israel, I had made my way to the United States, with a suitcase and what amounted to about one hundred dollars in my pocket.

My father, after World War II, had tried to rejoin his two brothers, who lived in New York City, but a strict quota had prevented him from getting the proper papers. He had stubbornly boarded a boat clandestinely, but upon arrival at Ellis Island, he was discovered and sent back to France. I joked often about the fact that he had tried to come to the United

States, but I had succeeded. We always had great fun and used to spend hours talking.

My mother was reserved, living in the shadow of his strong personality and accepting his mood swings that I believe were driven by World War II post-traumatic stress disorder, otherwise known as PTSD. In World War II, PTSD was known as combat stress or combat exhaustion, and the common belief was that the symptoms would resolve when the soldier would be removed from the war zone.

Today we know of the struggle to integrate in society these warriors face every day when they come home. My father was my hero, and despite our many disagreements and his irrational tempers, I thought he was the heart of our family. I know now that my mother was the glue that held us together, and I am sorry that I did not give her the credit for it sooner.

I was thankful they had both made the long voyage from France to be with me, and I was proud to walk down the hall holding on to my father's arm, as I was starting a new chapter in my life yet again. I was officially and willingly tying my life to a person who had in many ways a totally different personality from mine. Give and take was always the recommendations my elders had given me. I had pronounced the wedding vows with certainty in my heart and fear in my soul, and I knew I would have to bend, give, and change some of my ways to make it work. His laid-back personality and our friendship and love would do the rest. Our mutual sense of adventure fed our life, and we continued to experience nature and friendship through our many camping trips and gatherings.

Jake's bow matched the groom's.

My career was taking shape, but Allan was still struggling in the oil industry's ups and downs. He started considering other career options. When he landed an offer to work in Saint Thomas in the Virgin Islands, he was so delighted that I had no choice but to put my career aside and follow him. It was such an exciting opportunity for him, I wanted to be supportive. We decided that he would go first, find a home to rent and start working. I was to pack everything, get all our furniture shipped, and Jake and I would follow soon after.

During our transition, Jake and I would stay with a friend, until all loose ends were taken care of. We ended up at a coworker's apartment with a teacup poodle named Mister-T, who had the need to own and dominate everything around him. While Mister-T would prance around, Jake would sit or lie down quietly and tolerate the little guy climbing all over him. It was very apparent that he did not enjoy being hassled, but we were guests, and somehow Jake understood I wanted him to be nice. Mister-T went as far as to mount Jake's front paw to relieve his testosterone urges while Jake was lounging on the living room floor.

I would get to Mister-T as fast as I could, tapping his flank with one finger to snap him out of the mood he was in, but he would return a few minutes later, choosing the other leg as the subject of his obsession. Jake would sometimes just get up and walk around with the little guy tailing him, and I would inevitably excuse ourselves for Jake to find refuge in the small guest bedroom we occupied.

Jake and Mister-T while we waited to move to Saint Thomas.

Then came the week of our departure. I reluctantly quit my job and said good-bye to everyone I knew and finished packing my bags. Even though I was nervous about Jake's trip in the cargo bay of the plane, his quiet demeanor was putting me at ease.

The flight from Houston to Miami went by fast, but my worry about Jake kept me on edge. We had to change planes in Miami to head to Saint Thomas, and the time in between flights did not allow for a visit. I had read stories of dogs who got misplaced during layovers or even died when something went wrong with the environment in the cargo bay. I was thinking of the worst scenarios I had read, and I was slowly becoming a real nervous mess. So, I decided to close my eyes, breathe deeply, and visualize Jake calmly resting on his bed, his eyes closed. I could hear in my head the air raising his chest up and down, and my fingers could feel the soft fur around his powerful neck. I was smiling, and soon I was slowly falling into a quiet sleep.

The sound of the captain's voice, finally announcing our descent to Saint Thomas airport jerked me out of my sleep. My first thought went to Jake, and I was impatient to reach him and make sure he was fine. Exiting the plane was a slow and laborious process, but once out, I rushed anxiously to the luggage belt conveyor and waited for Jake's carrier. After fifteen minutes, there it was, coming along with the rest of the suitcases. As soon as I opened the carrier, Jake came out, wagging his tail and sniffing around, as relaxed and happy as can be. He had gone through two flights in a loud cargo bay and was as content as if he had just come out of a good nap in his own bed.

Now that my worry was gone, I waited with Jake for my luggage. Looking around I realized that Saint Thomas airport resembled pretty much a third-world-country airport, and I felt a little uneasy. I remembered landing in Tel-Aviv in Israel years before, in a country under constant daily terrorist attacks, feeling proud and invincible, but now in the small airport of Saint Thomas, I had butterflies in my stomach and was feeling vulnerable. I shrugged off the uneasiness that had invaded me, and after picking up my suitcase and reuniting with Allan, the three of us headed out, happy to be together once again.

The island was beautiful, lush and green with exotic flowers growing wild all along the roads. However, as we got deeper into the rain forest, I noticed that some of the houses were falling apart, with broken windows and washed-out doors. Large piles of trash layered some of the streets, and chickens were running free, eating the garbage.

The back of the island had been claimed by people who had little regard for the beauty of nature and who tried to simply survive at all costs. We were young and ignorant of what the future held; we just wanted to live in paradise, and unfortunately the best way to achieve our goal had not been discussed or investigated thoroughly.

The house Allan had found was on the top of a hill, in the rain forest away from town in the back of the island. Our neighbor was a Dutch man, who was growing fruit trees and flowers in a large colorful nursery abundant with exotic plants. The entrance to our yard was a massive rustic gate. The ground was basically gravel with not much vegetation, which seemed odd to me considering the beautiful green space our neighbor had. The view from the yard was that of the amazing blue ocean and two small islands. It was breath taking and I was hoping our home would be cozy and clean!

Entering the house was a sobering experience. The carpet was soiled, and the curtains were torn. Every fixture in the house seemed to be held together by a thread, and all was dirty and rusted. What was Allan thinking when he chose this house for our family? The two-bedroom, one bath house monthly rental was too much for our now single-income family, so his friend Patrick occupied one room and shared the expense with us. This house was the only place with a yard, Allan could afford. He had already signed a six-month contract with his job and could not back out.

I was unhappy that he had let me quit my job in Houston, and by now our furniture was most likely in transit somewhere in the vast ocean. I was regretting already all the decisions we had made together without investigating properly the island's real-estate options. Jake did not seem to mind the house and yard condition; he was with me and that was all that seemed important to him. How amazing would it be to live one day at a time, enjoying the moment for the simple things that made us happy without worrying about anything else. For my part, I couldn't possibly match Jake's capacity for happiness in this circumstance. I was livid!

A Wise Dog Named Jake

The next day we left Jake in the yard, and Allan took me to town to rent a car before going to work so that I could search for a job immediately. The plan was to be able to afford a better and safer place, and we needed two incomes to accomplish our goal. I picked up a small car and headed toward the business and shops area. There were so many cars and pedestrians that I opted to drive one city block behind the waterfront cafes. Cars were parked on both sides of the street and I had to drive slow with no more than a few inches of clearance on each side.

I was searching for an available parking space when a man jumped on my car, his dreadlocks slapping the windshield, his belly flat on the hood, and his black shiny eyes staring right at me. "Missy, stop!" he was screaming, holding on to the side of the car. I stared into his eyes, my heart jumped in my throat, and within a split-second, I knew I was in danger. My brain was foggy. I could hear the beat of my heart pounding into my ears, and then it happened! My right foot pressed hard on the accelerator pedal; the tires screamed on the hot pavement, and I heard the man roll over the hood of the car. Rows of parked cars flew by each side as I was desperately trying to get away. I watched the man in my rearview mirror jump back on his feet like a cat. He lifted his fist in my direction. I could feel his angry eyes following me. I did not stop the car until I got in front of our gate.

My mind was still racing, I was shaking and still sitting in the car trying to regain my composure when a knock on the window sent me jumping in my seat. "Sorry to startle you," a man said, staring at me.

Again, my heart was beating fast, and I could almost taste the adrenaline in my mouth. The individual introduced himself as my neighbor and added, "Your dog does not like shady people coming too close to your gate." What had happened? What was he talking about? Was Jake OK? Still sitting in the car, I searched for Jake, panicking, scanning the yard, and soon I saw him, behind the massive gate, wagging his tail and waiting patiently for me to come out of the car. I exhaled in relief and continued my conversation with my neighbor.

He explained that a man with long dreadlocks and wearing only shorts had come around the property, going back and forth in front of the yard fence while Jake was watching him from afar, quiet and hidden from view. When the man touched the gate, Jake had gone totally insane, throwing himself against the wooden gate and chewing it feverishly to get to the man, who evidently ran away as fast as he could. I could not believe what the Dutchman was telling me. It was scary to know that while my day had gone totally wrong, Jake's day had gone awry as well.

I told my neighbor what had happened to me in the street. He listened with a concerned look on his face, and he congratulated me profusely for not stopping and for getting rid of the man, whose intentions were most likely not friendly. The Dutchman was very animated about the danger that I had faced that day. As I walked through the gate and hugged Jake, I noticed all the scratches and the huge chunks of wood missing from the inside of the gate. The destruction was incredible! A chill went through my body. We were on the "bad" side of the island, danger was everywhere, and Jake knew it!

My heart was telling me that I needed to go back home as soon as possible, get my old job back in Texas if possible and bring my family where it was safer. The following days I reluctantly went to a couple of job interviews to please Allan, but with no industry on the island, I was reduced to putting my technical career on hold and trying to get a sales job in a tourist shop. No one was hiring, and it was very clear that we could not stay on the bad side of the island very long. We agreed that with only one salary, it would be difficult to move anywhere on the island acceptable for a couple with a large dog.

After several discussions about our options, Allan and I decided it was not a good idea to stay longer than needed in Saint Thomas. The next day I called my old boss in Houston, but as I suspected, he had already found a replacement for my position. However, he graciously offered to let me work part time until I could find a permanent job. The decision was made; I would wait for the furniture to arrive in Saint Thomas and arrange for it to be returned to Houston. Then Jake and I would fly back home and get organized. At the end of Allan's contract, he would come back home.

The few weeks I spent in Saint Thomas waiting for the furniture to arrive were somewhat pleasant. Jake and I explored together beautiful beaches and coves. One morning we stumbled upon a secluded beach, where a few stray dogs were hanging out. Jake was running off leash in front of me. He stood in attention for a moment, staring at a brown dog, most likely the leader of the pack. They both looked at each other for a short time. Jake's tail went up and started wagging slowly; he held his head high and calmly trotted toward the brown dog. Their body stances were identical; they were inquisitive but not aggressive. The tail wagging became more rapid as they started their ritual of sniffing each other and communicating their mutual respect and acceptance. Jake took a step back and bounced playfully in the air. This was the signal for all the dogs to play and run together.

I had just witnessed perfect strangers meeting on a deserted beach, initiating friendship and understanding, creatures that most describe as inferior to humans, yet who are wiser and more honest in their social behaviors. I was thankful for the time I was spending, observing their body language and the discussion that was intently creating the bond between them. The white sand was warm under my feet, and as I watched Jake and the pack run from one side of the small cove to the other side, I couldn't help but wonder if he would be happier living free with the pack on the island.

We came back to visit Jake's new friends several times. I would throw coconuts in the waves for them to chase after. Jake looked so wild; it was incredible to see him run side by side with the strays on the white sand, rushing through the waves and wrestling like old friends. His exuberance gave me a feeling of freedom and happiness. I felt safe, as if the cove was our sanctuary.

A Wise Dog Named Jake

Jake running with the pack of strays.
Jake is in the middle behind the brown dog, the
leader of the pack.

Brigitte Finkiewicz

Jake jumping in the waves after a coconut.

A Wise Dog Named Jake

Jake just being Jake, free as the wind, running toward me as if to say, "Look at me, I am having so much fun!"

Chapter 3

Getting Back Home

Jake and I arrived in Houston before the furniture. We spent a couple of weeks sleeping on the floor before it was delivered. Jake seemed to enjoy having me curled up next to him on the carpet all night long. I felt safe with him, listening to the quiet sound of his breathing in the dark and feeling the warmth of his fur against me. I would watch him at times as he was lost in his dreams. His legs would twitch, his breathing would intensify, and his eyes moved under his eyelids. Was he back in Saint Thomas running on the beach with the pack of dogs?

He was not meant to be confined to a small one-bedroom apartment. In fact, I had to convince the rental agent to bend the rules about the forty-pound dog size limit, written in the lease agreement. Jake was a healthy seventy-five-pound dog, but he was quiet and well behaved, so when I walked in the rental office with him, the women working there decided he was just a little over forty pounds. I thanked them with a smile and signed the lease while they were all loving Jake and laughing about all the kisses he was giving them. Jake was a charmer! I knew it would be just a transition until we found a house with a large yard for Jake, but for now, we were going to make this small apartment our home.

One evening, Jake and I set out for our usual last

walk before bed time. The apartment complex had a grassy area dedicated for dog walking, in the back of the buildings. It was a dark night, so I could barely see the fence that was running along the back of the grassy area. Jake was off leash, enjoying freedom, roaming and sniffing at every bush. I was walking slow, staring into the darkness without a thought, without a worry. Suddenly Jake took off and disappeared into the night with a bear growl that sent chills down my back. His tenacious bark resonated in the night, followed by a male voice screaming desperately, "Get your dog, get your dog!"

My heart jumped in my chest. I still could not see where Jake and the man were. I followed the screams in the dark, the adrenaline pumping through my veins. When I reached Jake, he stood tall, a few feet from the fence, chest out, his teeth shining in the night, the hair on his back raised up, and drool foaming from his mouth. I had never seen him with such anger and determination; it was frightening.

He was facing a tall dark man I had never seen before, who was clinging to the fence, staring with horror at Jake and begging me to hold him back. What had this young man been doing in the darkness before Jake found him? Was he stalking me, and because Jake was off leash away from me, did he think I was alone and vulnerable?

My mind was filled with terrifying questions; my blood was boiling, and my heart was beating so fast that my hands were trembling. I grabbed Jake's collar, composed myself as well as I could, and addressed the man in a stern voice, "You should NOT sneak up on people in the dark like that! I am not sure how long I can hold my dog back, you better be going."

"Yes, ma'am," was the last thing I heard from him, as he disappeared into the darkness.

I realized as I was following his shadow fade like a ghost in the night that I had stopped breathing. I inhaled deeply as if I had just emerged from water, bending over, almost nauseated. Jake was standing by my side, quiet and focused, still looking toward the darkness. I kneeled down and put my arms around his strong neck; burying my face in his soft thick fur, I said softly: "Thank you, my guardian angel. You are a good dog!"

Several studies have shown that violence against women is rampant in many countries including the United States. Penn, Schoen and Berland Associates conducted a telephone survey of 612 adult women between June 17 and June 19, 2000. They found that 87 percent of American women in the age range of eighteen to sixty-four had been harassed by a male stranger during their life, and over one-half of them experienced "extreme" harassment, including being touched, grabbed, rubbed, brushed, or followed. Every ninety-eight seconds an American is sexually assaulted, and every eight minutes that victim is a child; meanwhile only six out of every thousand perpetrators will end up in prison. A 2014 survey conducted by the Centers for Disease Control and Prevention reports that 19 percent of women in the United States have been raped at least once in their lives.

That evening I curled up next to Jake, with a

strong feeling that without him, I would most likely have been another number on one of these surveys. Even though I was married, I was too often living alone and, thus, most likely to be a victim of aggression. I decided that learning self-defense was the first step to take control of my environment.

Allan had mentioned his desire to start training in karate when he returned home, and I thought it might be a challenging and fun activity to do together. After researching the Houston area for different martial art clubs, I stumbled on to an organization called American Society of Karate, which also taught in different area schools, one of them close to home. I started training to empower myself and to help me deal with some of the challenges living alone brings. Karate and aerobic dance became a part of my weekly regimen. I could feel myself getting stronger and bolder not only physically but also mentally.

By the time Allan came back to Houston, Jake and I had made a home in our small apartment. We went on long walks and visited old friends together. Our life had a nice rhythm, and I was ready for my family to be reunited again. I had found a full-time job nearby and was ready to support my family until Allan could organize himself.

We settled fast into our new life, and every chance we got, we went wild camping so that Jake could be off leash. The beach was only one hour from our apartment, and Bolivar Peninsula was deserted from October to April. We would pack our tent, our homemade shower and water barrel, our camping toilet, and everything we would need for a few days' adventure. Crabbing seemed to be Jake's favorite activity. Of course, sometimes he showed more interest in the chicken neck to bait the crab than the catch itself, but we had fun, and dinner often consisted of fish or crabs we had caught.

One evening, while we were sitting by the fire near our tent, we noticed a large 1970's Cadillac making donuts at one end of the beach. We watched the car driving dangerously near the water, splashing and turning abruptly toward the beach to yet turn again making a figure eight in the sand. We commented that the driver would eventually get his car stuck, making such a racket. Just before we went in the tent for the night, we noticed the same car sitting in the sand. From afar, we could see the silhouette of a man sitting at the steering wheel, smoke escaping from the window in small regular clouds. We knew Jake would keep an eye on him. We did not worry, and we also knew the tides would be coming up very soon and he would have to move.

The night was bright with stars; the moon was high, and Jake had insisted on staying on guard outside the tent, so we settled in, and snuggled into our sleeping bags, content to still see the stars through the netted window in our tent. In the dark, the stranger from the Cadillac started slowly walking toward us, dragging his feet and squeezing a short joint between his fingers as he took deep hits. Jake was watching, his head down between his front paws, but his eyes wide open, scanning the darkness, and his ears erect, flickering at every noise.

When the man reached our perimeter a few yards

from our fire, Jake stood with a growl, followed by a ferocious bark, which sent Allan and me immediately onto our feet. "Excuse me, can you help me?" the man was muttering under his drunken breath. He was so inebriated that he was totally oblivious to the large black-and-brown dog growling and circling around him.

I calmed Jake down so we could hear what the man had to say. He explained his car was stuck in the sand on the other side of the beach and the tide was rising fast, and by now the water had most likely reached half way up his tires. Allan grabbed his keys and jumped into his truck, the man leading the way, to pull the Cadillac out of the water and up by the road, where the man spent the night sleeping off the alcohol and drugs he had consumed. By morning he was gone, and the beach was again ours alone to enjoy.

Jake and I relaxing during a camping trip on the beach.

A Wise Dog Named Jake

At the end of 1988, Allan and I decided to buy our first house. Every day after work, we would meet at our apartment, load Jake in my car, and drive to the location where our real-estate agent wanted to show us a home. Most of the time we came back home confused and a little annoyed that nothing we could afford was pleasing to us.

One Sunday afternoon we went without our agent, after hearing about a house for sale. It was a cute craftsman home, in a small modest neighborhood, close to my work. The side sliding door was unlocked, and we decided to sneak a peek. We immediately stepped into the dining room, with archways opening to the kitchen straight ahead of us and to our left inviting us to a large living room with vaulted ceilings, numerous large windows, and a massive fire place. It was bright with natural light flowing into each space with a warm welcoming glow.

We felt immediately at home. It was such a cute house, and already we were both thinking how we could remodel it to make it ours. We walked through every room, discussing with excitement what could be done for each area. Eventually we ended up in the back yard where Jake was wandering around, smelling every inch, marking his territory. It was a nice size yard, with plenty of room for running, playing, and even gardening. The next day, we called our agent, and we started the process of buying our first home. Little did we know this house would be our sanctuary for ten years, a place to grow together and pursue our dreams.

By the end of 1990, Allan had changed from an

offshore uncertain career to a steadier construction job in town. One winter afternoon he watched from afar several workers throwing rocks at a small animal. When he arrived at the scene, he realized the terrified creature was a small puppy who had escaped into a culvert pipe. In the darkness, he could hear the puppy cry.

He diligently crawled into the pipe, talking softly as he got close enough to reach and pull the frightened dog out. It was a little female, barely two months old, some type of black-and-brown hound, with floppy ears and a sweet little brown face. He took the pup in his truck and wrapped her in his coat on the front seat; she fell asleep immediately, feeling safe and warm.

When I got home that evening, Jake did not greet me at the door as usual; instead he was sitting by the kitchen doorway, staring inside the room. I could hear Allan talking quietly. I was not aware of the adventure of the day, but when I turned the corner to enter the kitchen, I discovered the subject of Jake's attention.

She was so skinny, still shaking a little after the bath Allan had given her; her little head and eyes turned toward me when I walked into the room. For a moment she just stared at me quietly. I could not resist taking her in my arms to warm her up and comfort her. By then, she had already entered my heart and made her little bed right in the middle of it. "She is no bigger than a peanut," I heard myself saying. "Peanut" became her name, and Jake instantly became her big brother.

She would jump on the sofa and wait for him to

come by and would literally fly onto his back to startle him. Jake would let her wrestle him down to the floor; he would lie on his back, teaching her the "kill bite" while she proudly would attempt to put her little mouth around his big neck to simulate the kill. Then it was the happy run through the doggy door and into the yard, where they would frolic until one of them would drop to the ground, tired and satisfied, resting for a moment until the urge to run again would possess them, and it was madness for a few more minutes of pure joy.

The weeks that followed her rescue I became Peanut's surrogate mother; the bond was undeniable. It was very apparent that she was wary of men, even of Allan who had rescued her, so she would spend most of her time following me like a little shadow. The drawback of such an attachment was the anxiety she suffered in my absence.

I returned home one day to find a living room full of beige fabric and little pieces of foam on the entire floor. My favorite recliner had been chewed all the way to the wood frame. When I entered the room, Jake just stayed in his bed, looking in the other direction, as if to say: "Don't look at me, I have nothing to do with that mess!". On the other hand, Peanut was coming toward me, twisting her little body, walking sideways, wagging her tail nervously, and looking up at me with her round guilty eyes.

Pets' destructive behavior is one reason their owners return them to shelters or outright abandon them in the street. There is no system in place to track the number of dogs or other pets that are abandoned each year in the United States; however it is known that between six to eight million companion animals are brought to shelters each year. Mahatma Gandhi said: "The greatness of a nation and its moral progress can be judged by the way its animals are treated." I believe he was right, and we have a long way to go to achieve the greatness he was talking about.

Dogs have been our companions for thousands of years; they depend on us for food, shelter, guidance, and love. When we adopt a dog, we become their pack, and when the leader of the pack leaves the den to hunt in the wild or in my case to go to the office, the rest of the pack adults follow to help in the hunt, while the offspring stay close to the den and wait for their return. With that in mind, we created an enclosed area just for Peanut, where she still could see Jake, roam around, and do her business, but did not have access to our furniture.

Dogs, like wolves, are den animals, so being in a small cozy space is a natural way that wolf pups grow up in the wild. We realized that Peanut felt safe in that space, and her anxiety subsided gradually.

Every day when I came home from work, my priority was to take both dogs for a walk and have them run and play for at least thirty minutes to one hour. Draining dogs' pent-up energy with exercise will calm them down and will help achieve better results in training.

Peanut was growing fast. Training was essential to keep the harmony in our home. As soon as she would understand what I wanted of her, the panting would go away, and she would display a more relaxed and happy behavior. When I approached a new lesson, she would become anxious again, most likely because of the confusion. Repetition was our friend in teaching her all the new commands.

Dogs are basically eager to understand us and be a part of our pack. Jake's communication skills were much easier for her to understand than mine, so observing him, I learned to use body posture and hand signals together with verbal cues. She progressed rapidly.

Peanut in the first week she came to live with us.

A Wise Dog Named Jake

Jake and Peanut were best friends instantly.

Brigitte Finkiewicz

Jake and Peanut resting, always near each other.

Puppy Love

Few months had gone by since Peanut came into our life, and despite the incredible amount of destruction that little puppy had caused early on, we loved her and continued working with her to build her confidence. When we would go for a walk, Peanut would put her little paws so close to my feet I had to be careful not to step on her. Jake seemed to always keep a watchful eye on her; I suppose he could sense her vulnerability, and as a good pack leader, when I was away or occupied with other activities, he felt responsible for her safety.

One weekend the morning ritual of her front paws drumming the side of the bed to wake us up fell silent. I must have moved around, for Jake to come to my side of the bed and nudge me with his nose. I woke up, and the silence in the bedroom ignited a fearful feeling that something was not right. I looked over at Peanut's bed; she was on her side, breathing quietly. Maybe she was just growing up and was losing her puppy morning ritual.

Lying quietly in bed, I could not shake the strange feeling that something was wrong, and Jake had his big head flat on the bed, staring at me relentlessly. "OK, big guy, I am getting up," I muttered in my morning breath. I sat up on the side of the bed and petted Peanut to wake her up. Jake was watching quietly. I shook her a little to get her to respond; she was still not moving, she seemed to be in a deep sleep. I tried to wake her up again, but to no avail.

Anxiously, I woke Allan, and by the time he was getting dressed, I had already called the clinic. We left Jake behind and rushed Peanut to her doctor. She was still unresponsive when we arrived at the clinic. A few hours later, the doctor had stabilized her and sent her home with an IV in her front leg. He was as puzzled as we were about her sudden condition, so he made arrangements for us to take her to a specialist for further examination.

The following week we visited the clinic our vet had referred us to. The specialist had to keep Peanut the whole day to run several tests. I was anxious; my stomach and my chest felt tight, and at times I caught myself taking a deep breath to calm down. It was a long and miserable day. Finally, I went back to the clinic, and they immediately brought me to an examination room where Peanut was recovering on a soft blanket. She had a small incision on her belly where they had done a biopsy. I curled up next to her and waited for the physician. The diagnosis was grim. Peanut was born with a liver a quarter of the size her body needed, so the impurities in her blood were not being filtered properly. Toxins had built up, and she had gone into a "liver coma," where her body had poisoned itself. The antibiotics had helped her fight the infection and she was feeling better, but it would happen again, and we were told that usually dogs with these health problems did not survive more than six months after being diagnosed.

The news hit me like a hammer thrown forcefully into my guts. I felt nauseated with pain; she was still so young! I held her in my arms, desperate to make the nightmare go away, trying to keep my wits to question the doctor as much as I could to make a plan and gain hope. Over the next few weeks, I watched her intently to familiarize myself with her body language and demeanor, in the hope that I would immediately notice when her system would go on overload, before she went into a coma.

Every few months for the first two years, she needed antibiotics to clear infections. Under my watchful eyes, she would bounce back very fast to be Jake's best friend again and run and play as if nothing was wrong. She grew into a beautiful forty-five-pound little hound, with an endless need for love.

The years passed, her health problems seemed to have gone away, and our life was full of joyful activities. Every day Jake and Peanut would await my return from work to go walking around our small neighborhood. On the weekend we would go camping, fishing, or entertain at home. Whatever the activities, Jake and Peanut were always a part of all the fuss.

The next morning, after a long night holding Peanut's leg IV in my hand following our visit to the vet.

Jake, Peanut, and I at a camping site. Peanut lying under my feet as always. Jake staring at the camera.

We did not think we would have another Christmas with Peanut, but she fought like a champion, and her health improved.

Chapter 4

Rescue Me...

I was driving by our neighborhood playground; children were playing with a black dog. He was running free from one child to the next; they were laughing and hugging and loving him. I was worried a little about the dog, because he was not restrained, and at rush hour, many drivers on their way back from work passed by the playground, people eager to get home, sometimes not respecting the speed limit.

I took Jake and Peanut on their daily walk later than usual that day. The children had gone home, and the dog was not at the playground. I figured he had gone home with one of the children. We walked our usual route, and on the way back home, at the corner of our street, Jake's head and ears went up. He stopped for a minute and pulled toward the other side of the road. The black dog was lying across the street by the sidewalk, looking at the cars passing by, but when we tried to approach him, he ran behind a bush. Was he a stray? He was so friendly at the playground. I was sure it was the same dog.

The next day I decided to investigate. The kids in the neighborhood told me that in the morning the dog would play with them until the school bus left, and then he would return to the spot by the side walk, a block away from the playground. They believed he stayed there all day until the kids came back from school.

Every day, I watched him stare at the cars that went by, waiting for something, waiting for someone. A neighbor told me they had seen the car driving away. The black dog had been dumped at the corner of our street, and he had returned to the same spot to wait for his owner. He would not let any adult approach him; only children could hug him.

I started feeding him regularly to get him used to me, in the hope that one day soon I would be able to get him to follow me home. Each day when I came to feed him, he would stare at me from afar, backing up at any movement forward on my part, so I would step away, squat down, and watch him devour the meal that I had left on the sidewalk. I would talk to him quietly while he ate, so that he would associate my voice with the warm feeling in his tummy, but he insisted on staying in the same spot, never losing hope that his owner would come back for him.

A week later, on my way from work, I had decided that I would ask the neighborhood kids to bring him to our yard, but when I came home that day, the dog was not in the playground with them. I decided to walk around the corner where he usually stayed. He was there, flat on his side, panting and obviously hurt. I assumed he had been hit by a car, and my heart ached, and the tears came flowing from my eyes.

I bent down by the sidewalk, a few yards away from him, talking to him softly, and to my surprise he came to me, dragging his right hind leg. I sat on the ground whispering and petting his soft head, running my hand gently around his body, trying to feel for inflammation or worse. His whole right side seemed painful. He looked into my eyes, following my every move, yet tolerating my touch and even lying against me.

When I got up, he painfully rose to his feet and walked behind me, step by step, dragging his injured back leg, while I encouraged him to keep going. We were just one yard away from our house, and yet, I could see the tremendous amount of courage he needed to move forward.

Jake and Peanut greeted us quietly, gently sniffing at the new arrival. He just kept his head down and stood silent, accepting respectfully the inspection. Jake and Peanut obviously understood the pain he was feeling, so they just rested next to him quietly, as if they wanted him to feel welcome and protected. I gave our new patient an anti-inflammatory pain medication for dogs with some food, and soon he felt a little better and looked content to have a warm bed with love and attention.

We decided to give our guest a name, and because of his beautiful black coat, I called him Coal. Coal would go to the clinic the next day, and hopefully get patched up, and we would keep him until a permanent home could be found. Coal was going to be loved, despite the cowardly and heartless previous owner who had abandoned him in the street.

The next day did not come fast enough, I could tell Coal was in pain, especially when he tried to get up. I worried all night about him. However, he slept well on a thick and soft bed we had made for him, but as usual my worry kept me awake all night.

The morning was hectic; I had to take Coal to the clinic and then turn around and drive the opposite direction to get to work. On and off throughout the day, I would feel a little pinch in my heart thinking about Coal and the heartbreak he had gone through, and now the battle he was facing to get better.

In the afternoon the vet called me to give me an update. He started with a solemn voice, telling me how much he really liked Coal and was thinking about adopting him. I could tell by the tone in his voice that the next sentence would start with "but…." And effectively, he continued our phone consultation telling me that the damage on Coal's hip, pelvis and leg was too extensive, and he thought that the best thing for Coal was to be put to sleep right now, while he was under sedation. The other option was to rebuild his pelvis, do a hip replacement and put a metal rod in his leg to attach all the fragments. Three costly and lengthy surgeries, which needed to be performed three months apart by a specialist and which would involve at least nine months of suffering for Coal with no guarantee.

My heart was suddenly invaded with sadness, faced with the fact I could not save Coal's life financially or ethically. Coal did not deserve to suffer any longer, but for one night he had been loved; he had slept in a warm bed, safe from the street and embraced by a family who wanted to help him. This was the end of the road for him and I felt terribly guilty I could not do more. Rest in peace, Coal, I did love you.

Coal's Legacy

After our experience with Coal and the realization that I had at home two dogs willing to accept strays without a fuss, I started opening my eyes to the streets of Houston. Several times I saw dogs walking on the road with their heads to the ground, scavenging for food. By the time I would make a U-turn, they would disappear behind a building, and I would lose sight of them. One evening on my way home, I noticed a little long-haired bird dog outside my neighborhood. She was so scared of people she had become aggressive, snarling at me when I tried to approach her.

I started bringing food to her location. Even though she would growl, she would wait at a distance for me to put the bowl down, and as soon as I would step back, she would rush to the food and swallow everything in a few seconds, keeping a wary eye on me at all times. There was a rope around her neck, and one end of it was dangling down to the ground, all chewed up. At some time in her life, someone had held her captive; she had chewed the rope to get away. She probably remembered how scary and mean that human was, and she did not want any part of me. Each day I would feed her a little closer to our neighborhood and then closer to our street, but I was never able to lead her to our backyard like I intended to, and she eventually disappeared to never be seen again.

On a sunny day, I was out by the garage cleaning my car when a little shaggy dog came walking down the street, no collar, no one around. She seemed to have appeared out of thin air. She was dirty but did not look skinny; someone must have been looking for her. I called her to me and took a leash and an old collar I had in the garage and walked her in the neighborhood, asking people if anyone knew whom she belonged to. She seemed friendly with all the dogs and people we were meeting, so I felt comfortable bringing her to the house. A bath was in order before I was going to introduce her to Jake and Peanut. She was very docile, and as I was scrubbing her back, she seemed to really enjoy my touch; she put her little scruffy face against my leg and closed her eyes in delight.

Jake was lounging on the living room floor and Peanut was lying on the sofa when we entered the room. They both jumped to their feet and came to greet us. There was a lot of tail wagging and turning in circles and bouncing around in happy gestures and sniffing each other, and then they seemed to settle down. I decided to make flyers and post them in the neighborhood as well as at my vet and other locations. A week went by, but no one came for her. We checked with the SPCA and the Humane Society to no avail. After a few weeks, we decided we needed to find a good home for her.

Working for a large company, I had an important network of people I could reach, and luckily enough, I found a wonderful couple who wanted to adopt her. The first visit was love at first sight. I had made my first rescue with my first home placement, and it felt good! Because of our sad experience with Coal, I had learned to act fast when a dog was lost. With Jake's and Peanut's tolerance, we were making a difference in not only the rescued dog's existence but in the life of her adoptive family as well.

So many times we see stray dogs in a street, but we are in a hurry, so we keep going, rationalizing that someone else will pick them up. Most strays in the United States will end up dying from injuries sustained when they collide with a vehicle or from disease such as, in the southern states, heart worms, a parasite brought on by mosquito bites, which invades the heart of the host until it cannot pump blood anymore.

The lucky dogs will be picked up and brought to a shelter before injury or sickness and might stand a chance to be adopted or euthanized humanely. Each year, approximately 2.7 million animals are euthanized in the United States (1.3 million dogs and 1.4 million cats). Of the dogs entering shelters, approximately 37 percent will be adopted, 33 percent will be euthanized and 30 percent of dogs who came as strays will be returned to their owners.

Brigitte Finkiewicz

The little shaggy dog meeting Jake and Peanut.

A Wise Dog Named Jake

We were encouraged by the successful rescue and adoption of the little shaggy dog, so our lives continued in the same rhythm, aware of the many blessings we had and the common rescue mission we now shared.

We noticed that most rescues we picked up were not altered. Over its life time, a female dog that is not spayed can have over a hundred babies, and males can literally father thousands. Unaltered pets are more likely to escape, roam, and get lost.

If every family in the United States rescued one dog or cat and got them fixed, in one year we would have prevented millions of unplanned litters and save as many as 117 million pets. A 1996 study shows that approximately 6.63 million kittens were born the prior year, 82 percent of which were from unplanned litters and 6.04 million puppies were born, 43 percent of which were from unplanned litters.

Tax-payers spend approximately 2 billion dollars annually to pick up, house, and euthanize homeless animals. The best way to reduce the number of strays is to increase spaying and neutering throughout the country by educating people about it and making it readily available to every household despite their social and financial status. The goal is to have only no-kill shelters.

Too many sweet and beautiful puppies and kittens are euthanized every week because of overpopulation and not enough homes to adopt them. This tragic reality weighed heavily on our hearts, so we continued to rescue year after year.

The stories in this chapter illustrate a few of the sweet babies we came across.

It was Halloween day, and I was busy decorating the front door for the many children who would ring the bell that evening when a little beagle walked down our street. I watched her trotting with her nose to the ground, expecting her owner to be right behind her, but no one appeared. I hurried toward her, squatted down, and called to her. She turned around and looked at me. I reached my hand out, and she came trotting toward me, with her tail high and ears erect.

As I grabbed her collar, I noticed that her behind and hind legs were doused in orange paint, but she looked otherwise healthy and friendly. On Halloween, many animals suffer abuse, but I had never heard of anyone spraying orange paint on a dog. We walked around the neighborhood, asking anyone if they knew the owner, knocking on doors, but to no avail.

I looked at the beagle who was quietly walking by my side; her collar held no information about her name or her previous address. "We'll call you Pumpkin," I told her, stroking her little head, and we went home. I was relieved to find that the paint was water based and after a shampoo, she was as good as new.

Pumpkin met Jake and Peanut with a cocky attitude. She pushed her chest against Peanut to make her back up, which Peanut did gladly, but Jake interfered with the same mannerism. He dominated Pumpkin in size, weight, and wisdom. He puffed his chest against her until she backed up with respect and stood immobile while he sniffed all over her.

A Wise Dog Named Jake

I was standing by the doorway, amazed at the conversation that was taking place silently in front of my eyes. Jake was basically telling Pumpkin that respect was to be observed in this house, and if anyone was going to push anyone, it was going to be him. As soon as Pumpkin gave in, Jake went to lie down, keeping a watchful eye on her.

Pumpkin and Peanut became good friends during the few weeks she stayed with us. Jake observed them play from afar, like a wise wolf supervising his pack from a distance to keep it safe and united. Pumpkin was adopted a month later by a friend of mine. She had been well behaved at our home, so we did not foresee any problem with the adoption. The months that followed, however, were difficult in her new home. Pumpkin went on a destructive rampage. It took patience and learning on the part of my friend to assert leadership and show Pumpkin that even though Jake was not at the new house she was to respect her human and new home.

I learned that with placing a dog comes the responsibility to support the new owner well after the adoption. I also learned that matching dominant dogs with first-time dog owners was challenging but, as Pumpkin's owner proved, not impossible. Dogs basically are social animals, and as such they look for leadership or will take the lead in their family or pack. A structured life with a regular schedule is important to a dog, like it is to a child, especially if he or she has just been welcomed into a new home. Dogs want to please their owner, but if family members send mixed messages, the dog will get confused, and "misbehave."

Pumpkin staring at the camera as she enters the kitchen.

A Wise Dog Named Jake

When Christmas came that year, the weather was reaching freezing temperatures for a week. Jake, Peanut, and I would take brisk walks around the neighborhood to come back with runny noses, eager to warm up in front of the fireplace, where a few logs were burning.

On one such walk, I noticed a small black poodle hiding behind a parked car. He was trembling, and his skinny body was hunched over, trying desperately to stay warm. I wrapped him in my scarf to pick him up. He went limp in my arms, his head finding the warmth of my neck. He did not move.

We hurried home, Jake and Peanut both lifting their noses in inquiry about the small package in my arms. When we entered the living room, I deposited with care the small poodle on a blanket in front of the fireplace. His eyes were half closed. He stayed immobile; he had barely the strength to lift his little head when Jake nudged him gently.

For two days and two nights, the small poodle lay on his blanket by the fireplace, except for eating and going to the yard for a short walk around. We decided to call him Tiny Tim. Soon after the holidays, I learned that Tiny Tim's owners had moved out of the house before Christmas and just left him outside to fend for himself. How could someone be so heartless, especially during the holidays when people are reminded to be giving and thankful. I was appalled, but I knew I could find a good home for him, and I did.

A wonderful family opened their heart to him. A sweet little girl showered him with love for months.

Unfortunately, Tiny Tim became sick, and despite the tremendous effort to save him, he had to be put to sleep. I was sad for the pain the whole family had experienced, but without each one of us getting involved, Tiny Tim would have never known about human's love and kindness.

Tiny Tim smiling at me.

One cold and rainy evening, on his way home, Allan noticed in the dark street a small dog trotting along the sidewalk. He stopped his truck as fast as he could, walked back to the sidewalk, squatted down, and called out to the dog. A little black cocker spaniel came rushing into his arms, wagging his little stump of a tail and whining in pleasure.

When they got home, human and dog were already bonded. She knew he was her savior, and she was not about to be lost again. For the weeks that followed, while we were trying to find her owner, she followed him around and spent most of her time in the garage with him or on the sofa next to Jake. She was a sweet little dog, but despite our efforts to find her owner, we were unsuccessful. Because of her black coat and the fact that she was found during a dark night, I called her Lilla, which means "night" in Hebrew.

Lilla became a part of our pack until I met a courageous woman, who had battled cancer but kept a cheerful attitude. She was in remission, enjoying every day of her life and wanting to share her time and love with a rescue dog.

One afternoon, she came with her daughter to meet Lilla. In an instant, you could feel the bond forming between the two of them. The cocker spaniel's little stub tail wagged frenetically as soon as the woman picked her up. It was undoubtedly meant to be.

There have been several research studies about the positive physical and mental effect pets have on people. Doctor Lynn Eldridge, an oncologist at the Mayo Clinic in Rochester, Minnesota, wrote: "A pet is a medication without side effects that has so many benefits."

Animals as companions to those with physical illnesses became recognized in United States only as recently as 1976 when Therapy Dogs International was founded, followed closely by the Delta Society. Their mission was to send volunteer teams and their personal pets to hospitals, nursing homes, psychiatric facilities, youth facilities, and much more to provide animal-assisted activities for therapeutic goals.

Today several organizations, in cities throughout the United States, have followed the path of Therapy Dogs International and the Delta Society. They provide the same therapeutic service well recognized in the medical and nursing care community. Research has also shown that owning a pet can reduce stress, anxiety, and depression, as well as ease loneliness and encourage exercise. Some studies suggest that interaction with a dog can lower blood pressure in older adults.

Lilla was the sweetest of our rescues, and her job started on the day she met her new owner, who had battled cancer.

A Wise Dog Named Jake

Over the years, a small dedicated group of co-workers helped us rescue over thirty dogs from the streets of Houston. We named our modest organization Best Friends Rescue. A company magazine posted an article dedicated to the people working together, to honor Coal, the black dog who patiently and loyally waited at the corner of the street for the owner who had abandoned him. The article states that "Best Friends Rescue was born to help the dogs, who for whatever reason, find themselves discarded like junk food containers on the side of the road." This was a sadly accurate description of our mission. Later that year, I wrote in a journal, about the strays I encountered and about Jake who had become their ambassador:

"They are out there, the unwanted, the maltreated.
They are hungry, lonely, and defeated.
Look in their eyes; reach out to them,
Open your heart; we do owe them!
We have tamed them for thousands of years,
To fill our empty souls and fight our fears.
They are our pets, our loyal friends,
Don't turn your heads; don't discard them!"

Coal had not died in vain; his spirit was alive in every wagging tail each rescue dog displayed when we gave them love and a warm place to stay. Jake was paying forward the goodness he had found in our home and worked diligently to keep the pack's harmony every time we brought a stray. Without him, I am not sure we could have done it so successfully

Chapter 5

Jake's World

As the years went by, Jake's age was starting to show. His muzzle had turned white, but his strength never wavered. He would walk around with a small soccer ball, anticipating the play. It's not so much that Jake was a good retriever; he loved the challenge of the chase and the hunt. When an occasional opossum would walk our fence line from the wooded area at the end of our street, he would be stopped by Jake's alarming barks and athletic jumps.

Usually the wild creature would go into a fainting trance and would just fall back to the other side of the fence, but one day, the creature somehow fell on our side of the fence, and Jake was facing it. The barking had ceased, and they just stared at each other. The opossum's long pointy teeth were very impressive. His mouth stayed open as he hissed and followed Jake's every move. Jake was focused and calm, moving from right to left, analyzing the creature's reactions.

He was preparing for the kill; the wolf from his ancestors was surfacing, and when he made his move, it was in a flash, and I realized the creature in his mouth was already dead. During the whole event, Peanut stood aside, watching quietly until the kill was accomplished, and she then came alive, like a wolf pup welcoming his mother after the hunt. I had witnessed the amazing power of nature.

I stood in awe, contemplating the scene when Jake slowly dropped the opossum's limp body in front of my feet. This was the ultimate present. I squatted down and examined the animal while Jake sat quietly, waiting for my praise. Even though I do not enjoy killing any animal, this was nature doing its best to keep the balance between predator and prey. I petted both dogs to convey my appreciation, and they wagged their tails in response.

Our house and yard were Jake's territory, and several times a day and at night, going through his large doggy door, he would patrol the grounds, like an old soldier guarding a fort from a potential attack.

I was at work when a friend of ours called me to let me know that he needed to enter our yard to retrieve the sunglasses he had forgotten the previous day on our picnic table. The only problem was that the gate was locked, and he would have to jump the fence to enter the yard. I thought it was safe for a friend whom Jake knew to enter the yard. Was I ever wrong!!!

Our friend climbed the fence without a problem and retrieved his sunglasses, but by the time he turned around toward the back gate, Jake was standing between the fence and him, all teeth bared out and barking ferociously. They stood there, staring at each other, like two old cowboys ready for a shootout.

My phone rang again, and he shouted at me: "Jake does NOT want me to get out!" I calmed him down and asked him to talk to Jake. They had played together the day before, Jake knew who he was, but like in Saint Thomas, he did not like the idea of someone coming around the fence uninvited. In his mind, a person without a key was not supposed to be there. After a quiet conversation with Jake, our friend jumped the fence and got away with just his pride a little bruised.

Jake's world included the house, the yard, Peanut and us, so no one else could come in unless Jake thought they were supposed to be here. Our cleaning lady would enter with her key, and after greeting her at the door, Jake would keep his distance. He was not too keen on the vacuum cleaner, but somehow, he had accepted the ritual of this person who invaded his space a few hours a week.

But when a phone company technician decided to jump the fence to verify the telephone box for a performance problem I had reported, Jake did not see his presence as an authorized visit. The phone rang in my office, and when I responded, the nervous gibberish that came through the line was almost comical. "This is Dave with the phone company.... Hmm.... I tried to go in your yard to verify your box, but your dog did not want me to approach the house.... Hmm...and he knows how to open the gate!" What was that story about?

Dave explained that he had jumped the back gate to enter the yard and walked toward the phone box, when Jake came out of the house and held him hostage on the spot. So he had tried to turn around and briskly run back to the gate with Jake on his heels. He had closed the gate behind him, but Jake had jumped on the latch and opened it. Jake was standing by the open gate, barking and looking at him as we talked, so the man was obviously shaken by the experience.

I had told the phone company of Jake's presence, and I had asked them to let me know when the technician would make the house call so that I could arrange to close the doggy door on that day. Unfortunately, they did not take the safety of their workers seriously.

"His name is Jake, and he is a sweet dog," I answered him, and I advised him to talk to him gently, so that Jake could understand he was supposed to be there. I encouraged Dave to let Jake come to him. He reluctantly complied. I listened to the conversation that was taking place in front of my yard between a stranger and a wise dog named Jake.

I heard the man say, "I just want to do some work Jake, good dog, good dog!" and I assumed Jake was sniffing the man and when the man made a slow move back to the gate, Jake followed him quietly and let him work, but Dave reported to me that Jake did not let him out of his sight.

Peanut apparently stayed in the house while Jake was dealing with the "intruder". From day one, Jake had been Peanut's protector. I am not sure if he had communicated to her to stay indoors, like a mother wolf keeping her young in a den during danger, but she always stood out of the way when there was danger, and Jake would always move forward toward the front line. The dynamic between the two was typical of the parent and the offspring.

His eyes would light up as soon as anyone wanted to throw the ball.

The Adventure Continues

We had bought a small ski boat, and we would pack for two nights of camping by Lake Conroe. In those days, there were still parcels of land that did not seem to belong to anyone. We had found a cove with an old abandoned dock, where we could tie our boat and spend a couple of days camping with the dogs. We loved the freedom it gave us; it would replenish our spirits, away from the bustle and hassle of city life. Peanut would lie down under my legs in between my seat and the console of the boat and Jake would stand at the bow, nose cutting the wind, straight as a statue, with his eyes half closed, enjoying the wind on his face.

One such day, we had started our voyage to the far side of the lake to find the cove, when the wind started to pick up, and within a few minutes, the water became dangerously agitated with rolling waves, slapping the side of the boat, splashing Jake violently as the boat went up and down.

Peanut was shaking against my legs. I tried to console her and protect her from the rain that had started pounding the boat relentlessly. Allan was busy maneuvering the boat and Peanut was too scared to be left alone, so Jake was facing the storm alone, still standing at the front of the boat, but by now he was looking around, and I could tell he was uneasy. I called him up to me, but the wind took my voice away from his direction, and he stood there confronting the weather, like an old captain directing his vessel through the roaring of an angry sea.

The storm lasted fifteen minutes and then went away as fast as it had come. When we reached the cove, the sun had come back, and the water was calm again. Peanut and Jake jumped onto the dock and ran around the cove, happy to be free and delighted to be on solid ground. We unpacked our gear and set camp near the water but hidden from view in the tree line. This cove was our little secret, our domain where Peanut and Jake could run free and where we could imagine for a weekend that we lived in the wild, eating food cooked on the wood fire and sleeping under the stars.

At nightfall, we would gather around the fire, Jake would lie next to me, his big head resting on my lap, enjoying my touch on his neck while I gazed into the starry sky. In the morning after a hearty breakfast, composed of scrambled eggs, toast and fresh fruits, we would sit by the water to fish, while we dreamed about someday having our own beautiful piece of land to escape to.

Eager to find our own paradise, we often adventured into an unknown pathway, such as the narrow and shallow canal we stumbled upon in Lake Conroe one July afternoon. The sun was relentless, and we were looking for shade when we arrived in what seemed like an overgrown canal, with tree limbs reaching the water and casting their wide shadows. We slowly drove the boat under the foliage, and finally relieved from the intense heat, we turned off the motor and dropped our boat anchor.

Jake and Peanut were relaxing near me on the

pillows that made the bow bedding, while Allan was sitting on the ladder in the back of the boat, splashing water on his neck. When he jumped in the water, he realized that it was only waist-deep. Incited by the idea to cool off, I decided to also take a plunge. Without a thought or worry, I entered the water and walked around to Allan.

Immediately I heard a splash beside me and caught a glimpse of Jake's tail sinking in the water like a submarine's telescope. When he came to the surface, Jake slowly pedaled his front legs to stay afloat near me. I decided to walk to dry ground, and he happily followed me while Peanut watched, nervously running from one side of the boat to the other.

Jake was heavy, and pulling him onto the boat would take too much effort. I decided that the ladder and the platform at the stern of the boat was the only effortless way to get him back inside the boat. I sat down for a few minutes to let him rest. Talking to Jake always had a calming effect not only on him but also on me. So, I discussed with him the plan I had to get him back on the boat, while Allan watched, shaking his head in dismay. "He can do it," I said, trying to convince him and myself at the same time.

I walked back into the water with Jake trailing me and made my way to the back of the boat. I climbed the ladder, stepped on the platform, and turned around to talk to Jake. He was already struggling to put his back feet on the first step, his front paws were stretched out on the platform. Allan gave him a push from behind, and Jake was back on the boat, shaking his whole body in delight and sending water spray all over us. "And that is how it is done!" I said with a laugh, throwing an amused look in Allan's direction. "I knew he could do it!"

Peanut and I fishing off the dock in the morning.

In November that year we spent a long week-end in Bandera, Texas, riding horses on a dude ranch. Having reserved our vacation off season, we were the only guests on the ranch, so we enjoyed our secluded cabin, with the peace that the hill country has to offer, with sightings of deer, rabbits, squirrels, several species of singing birds of many colors, and the ranch dogs keeping us company. Our cabin in the woods looked down onto a valley where horses ran free, and my dream of one day having my own horse farm floated incessantly in my head.

We had enjoyed every minute of our vacation, but it was time to get back home; we both had to work the next day. Our dog sitter had taken care of Jake and Peanut, and we were anxious to be reunited with them. When we drove up to our garage, in the brightness of the headlights, we saw a small black animal rummaging through our neighbor's trash. Immediately we realized it was a puppy.

We jumped out of the truck and went after the dog, calling softly. She came running to us, a little Rottweiler-boxer mix with a sweet face and wiggly body. It was already dark, and we knew she had to be lost or abandoned and needed our help. I could hear Jake and Peanut barking inside, excited by the sound of our voices and eager to see us. We thought the best way was to just walk in with the puppy as if she was a part of the plan and hope that Jake and Peanut would accept her immediately, despite their agitation.

The young dog was happy seeing other dogs, and her demeanor was friendly and respectful. Immediately she realized that Jake was the authority, and she gently licked under Jake's muzzle in submission as he towered over her. Both Jake and Peanut did a lot of sniffing, and she submitted to all the inspections. After a good meal, everyone settled down in front of the TV with us, and it looked as if she had always been a part of the pack.

The next day I decided to investigate. The best people to question were always the children on the playground; they seemed to know about the dogs in the neighborhood. The story I heard from several kids made me angry. A man had driven up to the playground; he had gotten out of the car with the puppy on a leash, removed her leash, gone back to his car, and methodically driven off without a word, without looking back.

The young dog had stayed the afternoon playing with the kids, but at nightfall, when everyone left, she had roamed alone, looking for food. She was safe now, with a full belly and a warm blanket, playing with Peanut, who had become a big sister to her already. The two seemed to grow inseparable very quickly. Jake would stay stoic as they ran circles around him. I decided to call her Xena, after a TV series that we were enjoying at the time.

A few weeks later, we put her up for adoption, but I could tell that neither of us was really convinced we could find someone "good enough" for her. We were falling in love with her. Peanut seemed to have gained back her puppyhood, and we enjoyed watching them wrestle and run around the yard together. Jake's pack had gained another member. She was here to stay!

Peanut and Xena resting after lots of running in the yard.

Chapter 6

Sorrow

By 1993, my father was battling a very difficult war, within himself. He had been diagnosed with Parkinson's disease a year prior and was at the very last stage when dementia takes a big part of one's short-term memories and replaces them with the long-term memories. His name was Mendel Finkiewicz, and for my siblings and me, he always had been a strong, smart, and loving father. It was hard to see him struggling to get up, his hands trembling, his eyes staring at an imaginary point in empty space. His voice had become a whisper, and he would fight to organize and express his thoughts.

He was born in Poland in a modest Jewish family, and because of the rampant anti-Semitism, he had emigrated as a young man, before World War II, from Poland to France. When the war started, not able to join the French army because of his emigrant status, on October 20th, 1939, he had signed up with the French Foreigner Legion, to combat the advancing German invaders.

On April 28th, 1940, during a battle in the French region of the Ardennes, he was taken prisoner and kept in the Stalag 12EA. The Stalag 12EA was one of Germany's largest prisoner-of-war camps, located near Metz in the north of France. During his incarceration, he was submitted to "special" treatment and pushed to work in the worst conditions because of his Jewish background. He endured physical and mental abuse, but his resoluteness carried him through the challenges to survive at all cost. The conditions in the camp were deplorable, and many prisoners would get parasites or infections. Despite the freezing weather, prisoner Finkiewicz kept healthy hygiene. Every morning he would strip down, rain or snow, and wash his body, even with snow if that was all he could use, to keep healthy and strong.

Before the war, my father was a tailor by profession. During his incarceration his craft would lead him to attempt an escape. He decided to sew civilian clothes with old blankets, working quietly at night in the moon light. Every noise and every shadow would send him into alert, and he would hide his labor, waiting in the dark, listening, barely breathing, and when all was quiet again, he would reach for his sewing kit and continue his work.

The day he wanted to escape, underneath his striped pajamas, he wore the suit, fabricated with care out of an old blanket. German guards lined up every prisoner in the snowed-in court yard for the morning roll count. All was going as expected; he planned to escape early during the day while working in the woods under the guards. He knew they would not count again until the evening before they returned to camp.

Something was different that morning; the German officer ordered every prisoner to remove his pajamas. Mendel realized that someone had reported him, probably to gain protection or acquire more food; it was desperate times, and some did the unthinkable to survive. The prisoners undressed, wary of the change in protocol, shivering in the freezing wind, but Mendel Finkiewicz was not cold. In fact, the temperature of his body was boiling. He knew his escape plan was discovered. The German officer stood in front of him, looking straight into his eyes, his face so close he could smell his rancid coffee breath. "Was ist das?" (What is it?) the officer yelled in German, pointing and grabbing at the clothing, while Mendel struggled to explain that he had made warm clothes because he was cold.

He was ordered to strip, and while everyone watched, he was questioned, tortured and questioned again, but he never changed his story: "I made warm clothes because I was cold," so they left him naked and battered in the snow for twenty-four hours. It was December, the nights were bitterly cold, so he curled up trying to retain some heat, talking and singing aloud to prevent his mind from shutting down. Every so often, when shivers would shake his whole body uncontrollably, he would get up and jump up and down and rub snow on his wounds and his body to make the blood in his legs and arms circulate again.

He survived the bitter cold night, and after allowing himself to heal and gain strength, a few weeks later, on January 5th, 1941, determined to find freedom, he attempted another escape, and this time he succeeded. He told me of that day: "I could hear the dogs barking way into the night, and I kept running."

To regroup, he went back to Paris, but his apartment was occupied by Germans, and the Vichy

Government, collaborating with the Nazis, had the gendarmerie (French Police) looking for him, so he decided to go to the Free Zone in the south of France, in Toulouse, where he stayed until November 1942.

Despite the underground fighting in the south of France, the German army invaded the region as well, so he chose to head out to Spain, to reach the Free French Army, commanded by Charles De Gaulle in Casablanca. In the village of Bourg Madame, close to the Spanish border, two Germans patrolling the area stopped him and held him at gunpoint. He stood with his hands up behind his head, thoughts of running racing through his mind, but he knew running was not an option; they would undoubtedly shoot him in the back.

Because he had no papers, they wanted to escort him to their headquarters, one soldier with a machine gun on one side and the other man with a side arm on the other side. He knew that if he entered the headquarters, they would find out he was Jewish. He had heard stories about German soldiers asking men with no papers to drop their pants so that they could see if they were circumcised or not. In Europe, Christians do not circumcise their baby boys. It was a sure way to found out if a man was Jewish.

He had also heard about the camps where they sent all the Jews, never to be seen again. He knew they were being exterminated, and he was ready to die here rather than being sent to one of these death camps. While they were walking toward the village, his mind went suddenly blank, and without any more thought, rage and fear took over; he pulled the small knife he always carried in the back of his shirt collar and plunged it into the first soldier's heart and swiftly turned to the second man before he could pull his gun out of the holster and inserted the blade into the German's neck.

Adrenaline pumping in his veins, Mendel Finkiewicz ran toward the Pyrenees mountains, leaving behind a bloody mess and the agonizing screams of the two men. He walked during the nights and rested during the days until he reached Barcelona, where he joined for a few months the Spanish underground while trying to get French papers from the French consulate. Unfortunately, the French consulate worked with the Vichy government, who worked with the Germans, and they arrested him on January 23, 1943, and sent him to a prison in Madrid. However, in April 1943, they released him with assigned French papers, and commanded him to stay in Madrid and report regularly. Motivated by the desire to join the Free French Army, he decided to run and reach Portugal to embark on a cargo boat, destination Casablanca. On June 3, 1943, he became a part of the 102nd regiment and was sent to Tunisia. My father fought during the campaign of Italy, and on August 14th, 1944, he came back to French soil with the first French army with whom he would fight until 1945, the end of the war.

During my visit in the summer of 1993, he was tormented by guilt, telling me about the German enemies, the war and all the shame that came with fighting and killing. He told me about the two young German soldiers he had killed on his way to Spain.

"They were kids," he whispered, with the painful guilt of a man who never forgave himself.

I tried to convey to him that during wars, one finds oneself in extraordinary situations that demand extraordinary actions. "Papa, if they had had a chance, they would have killed you, and I would not have been born. And you would not have helped free and rebuild France." It was so painful to realize that the father with whom I had laughed, cried, and grown had hidden the pain and the guilt of the hideous war he had survived.

That afternoon, after everyone but us had gone for a walk, he told me the stories that haunted him, and then he put his head on my shoulder and he cried softly, while tears rolled down my cheeks and I held him tightly: "You had no choice, Papa, you had no choice."

Besides the pain of the past, it was so sad to see him struggling with every step he took. The man who was my hero was barely holding up his poor, tired body and fighting to stay mentally coherent. "Look what I have become" were the first words he told me when I came into the room where he was standing holding onto a cane.

In April of 1994, I went back to France to visit him again, because he was hospitalized. During my visit, we had talked every day from morning to evening. Somedays were better than others, but at the end of my stay, when I said good-bye, I knew in my heart it was forever. Two weeks later my mother called me and told me he had died. My heart almost exploded when I heard these words. All I could say was: "He is not suffering anymore, I hope he finally found peace."

In June 1994, fifty years after D-day and fifty years after he landed on a southern beach of France with the first French army, I was burying my father with full honor, the French and Free French Army flags, floating softly in the wind, held by two of his comrades on each side of his coffin. Throughout the painful day, I held my tears, trying to stay strong for everyone around me and to honor the man, the father, and the hero.

My mother gave me his military papers, and even though so much information about his whereabouts during the war was written, I still needed to hear all the anecdotes he had told me but I had failed to record. The first year after he died, I often caught myself saying, "I'd like to know what Papa thinks about this or that," to realize that no more phone call was possible, and there would be no more sitting at the dining room table of the apartment where I had grown up in Toulouse, France, talking for hours about the war or about his life in Poland. He was gone!

However, I realized after going through the grieving process that a person will disappear only if his legacy does not survive the test of time. Mendel Finkiewicz was never "gone" because in my heart and my soul he still influenced the many facets of my life. The first lesson I remember happened when I was six years old. Papa and I encountered our upstairs neighbor, an old grumpy dentist who used to scream at us through the open windows of his apartment.

Papa was holding my hand as we made our way through the steep stairs leading to our third-floor apartment. The neighbor exchanged a few words with my father, and soon I heard his voice take a loud turn. My heart started pounding. I stood closer to my father who was still holding my hand, and I felt his grip getting tighter. "You dirty Jews," I heard the neighbor say to us in a threatening voice.

I looked up at my father and watched him lean over the man, their faces almost touching. He said quietly, "You are lucky my child is with me, or I would have shown you what a 'dirty Jew' can do to you!" His stare was piercing, and his presence was immense. The silence that followed told me that Papa had stood for the freedom of not being afraid and of always keeping our head up despite what the adversity might be.

This first experience shaped my life and molded my personality, and in the years that followed, my thirst to discover the fate of my father's Polish family became more urgent. So when I reached eleven years of age, my dad sat me down and showed me a book he had bought after the war. It was a huge hard copy, at least twenty inches wide, heavy with pages and pages of pictures and Yiddish writing. As he opened the book at one specific page he had marked, he pointed to the picture of an old couple and said, "This is your grandfather and your grandmother. She died before the war, but he was killed by the Nazis." Then his hand hovered to the next page where a young woman in her good Shabbat clothes was posing with her husband. "This is your aunt, my sister, who died in Auschwitz, as well as her husband." The book laid in front of me was about the Jews of his hometown, massacred by Hitler's SS.

A Wise Dog Named Jake

Papa told me about the families and the children he knew; each picture had a story: "This one lived down the street from me; we were friends. This one sat next to me in the classroom…." Then solemnly he turned to me and told me, "They killed all my friends, my family." He paused for a moment, looking far away beyond the wall of our apartment, and quietly continued, "Hitler wanted to annihilate the whole Jewish population, but he failed because we are strong and good people, and we have learned to survive adversity".

Throughout the years I learned so much from this incredible man who never once bent under pressure. He was tough and sometimes difficult to live with, but he was my hero, and I still pull strength from his presence inside of me.

When I returned home to Houston that summer I wanted to do something to honor him. I thought that volunteering, helping others, would help me deal with my own pain. I recalled reading about an animal therapy program in Houston, and I knew that it was the route I wanted to take. Jake was getting old, but Peanut had mostly grown out of her fear of men, and visiting patients would certainly boost her self-esteem.

In April 1995, she passed temperament testing to become a volunteer in an animal-assisted therapy program with an organization named Caring Critters. Caring Critters had been operating in the Houston area since 1988. Like Therapy Dogs International and the Delta Society, Caring Critter's mission was and still is today, to enhance the daily living of patients by providing interaction with pets. The group visits socially, therapeutically, and educationally, hospitals, retirement homes, crisis centers and much more.

Peanut and I started visiting an assisted-living facility. It was my way of dealing with my tremendous loss. Through the blurry eyes, the trembling hands, the smiling faces, and the whispering voices of the residents we were visiting, many times I caught a gleam of my father. My heart would start pounding for a second, and I would do a double take to confirm that it was not him. I wondered at times if he was not indeed there, playing tricks on me. Despite the terrible experiences he suffered throughout his life, Papa loved to joke around. He would tell a funny story to entertain us and laugh through his teeth, making the sound of a pneumatic door as it slowly closes with a hiss. I always told him he sounded like a bus door, and it made him laugh even harder. I cherish the good times we had together and all I learned from him.

Even though it has been decades since I have heard his voice, his presence is still with me, ever so strong and reflected with passion through this chapter to honor his memory.

Papa in his World War II military uniform.

Chapter 7

Life's Challenges

Life went on without my father and with the years passing by, I noticed that the pain that once had taken hold in my heart was slowly subsiding and laughter had come back to our home. During Christmas 1997, I caught the biggest, meanest flu I had ever suffered. My nose was running continuously, and my head felt like it was in a vise, tightened against my temples. I moped around the house until New Year's Day, spending most of my time in bed or on the sofa and getting up only to feed the dogs, Allan, and myself. Usually very active, it was unusual for me to get sick or even to slow down. Jake, Peanut and Xena spent the whole week by my side, quietly observing me with a sense of worry. Xena would tug at Peanut at times, and I could hear them going through the doggy door and frolicking in the yard; then they would rush back into the house, out of breath, and would plop down with a grunt, to lie quietly again next to my bed. Jake, however, did not seem to leave my side, and any time I opened my eyes, he was lying near me. If I just moved an arm, he would get up, put his nose flat on the bed, and stare at me inquisitively. I would say to him, "I am fine," to reassure him, or maybe reassure myself, that I would get better soon.

New Year's Day was a beautiful sunny winter day. I was feeling better, it was time to get dressed and breathe in the fresh air. We decided to drive and explore the area where we had seen beautiful parcels of land. I had rekindled my love for horses a few years earlier by taking care of and exercising a couple of friend's horses. Since the previous year, I had been leasing a young spirited Arabian gelding named Storm, and driving miles to ride him a few times a week. After countless challenging hours of training, he had won my heart with his untamed spirit, and I was thinking of buying him. Finding land, building a stable, and getting horses was a dream we shared, and little did we know that our ride that January 1, 1998, would lead us to the perfect place.

It was the wood-carved neighborhood sign, with the outline of a horse grazing peacefully, that got my attention as we were driving by. "Stop, turn around!" I yelled in anticipation. We made a fast U turn, and we entered the small neighborhood, with houses hidden behind thick trees and horse fencing around large paddocks, and then I saw the sign: "For sale by owner". It was meant to be; this was the perfect piece of land and the perfect neighborhood, tucked away but close enough to town and to my work.

I called immediately the number on the sign, and the man who answered the phone told me that he had just posted it three hours earlier. I had a great feeling about this place; this was going to be the beginning of a wonderful adventure.

In February of 1998, we became owners of a 2.5-acre parcel of land, where we started immediately to plan and build a horse stable with three stalls and one tack room on one side and a small apartment on the opposite side. I was ecstatic at the thought that I would have my horse and my dogs in a single location with us and that I would be able to ride every day if I wanted to, without having to drive elsewhere.

After we purchased the land, our life became much busier. Allan would leave the house on Saturdays after breakfast to start working on the stable with the help of a friend. I would stay at home with the dogs, clean the house, mow the yard, and by noon, I would prepare a lunch basket, load the dogs in my Explorer, and head out to our land. We would spend the rest of the day pulling nails out of reclaimed wood we were using to build our foundation or do whatever was on the construction schedule. Our Sundays were not much different, but every week that went by and each bit of progress we made was a step closer to the realization of our dream. Peanut and Xena enjoyed running free in the large pasture, and they would come back panting, wagging their tails and plunging their noses into the large water bowl as they slurped side by side, sending water everywhere around them. Jake, who was already as per our calculation nearly seventeen years old, would just lie down by a large tree and observe the activities from afar. I wanted all of them to be comfortable with the location so that the move would not be so dramatic. They seemed in their own individual ways to enjoy their days on our land, and I too was happy to see the joy in everything we did. Our farm was slowly taking form, and we had to pinch ourselves to process the reality that was taking place. It was the most exciting time of our lives together.

The first week I met Storm I knew I would fall in love.

Peanut and Xena enjoying their freedom on our land.

The stable taking form. This is the stalls' side before we painted it.

Storm running in our new arena

A Wise Dog Named Jake

While we were busy building, I was also teaching my horse Storm to load in a trailer, among other necessary lessons to come live with us. What I did not know about this magnificent animal when I started riding him was that he did not trust humans because of prior rough training he had endured. He was rebellious and unruly. That the first week I rode him he was on his best behavior, was most likely his way to learn all my weaknesses. The farmhand later told me that Storm bucked off every rider, and even the owner had been thrown repeatedly. I had always ridden ranch horses that were well behaved, so this little Arabian was a challenge for me.

I decided to take lessons so that I could have the expertise of a trainer. One such lesson day, I was riding Storm in the large arena; the trainer was standing in the center, directing the exercise. She asked me to go into a canter, which is a controlled gallop. I signaled Storm gently with my legs. In a flash he was galloping rapidly; every turn we made his speed increased. He was totally unresponsive to the pressure I was putting on the light snaffle bit in his mouth, and he ran away with me like a wild horse. I held my center of gravity; my thighs were holding tight against the saddle, but I could feel my feet losing hold of the stirrups, and at each lope my seat was coming forward, until the saddle was totally gone from underneath me, and I was riding on Storm's neck. Nothing I did to stop him worked. I was losing my balance, so I reached behind me, grabbed the back of the saddle with one hand, with the reins and his mane in my other hand, I jumped back on the saddle, pulling the reins tight as I was determined to stop him. To my relief, he stopped immediately and stood there, snorting with satisfaction.

The trainer and I decided it was time to teach him a lesson of perseverance. I made him work that day, and even when he was ready to stop we continued the exercises, until we both were wet with sweat. We finished our lessons with a slow sit-trot, where the horse trots so slowly the rider can sit comfortably without posting up and down. I had the feeling we were floating on air; it was such a wonderful feeling to have him gently following my commands. This was just the beginning of many difficult days of trying to convince a one-thousand-pound animal that I was not the enemy and we could have fun together if he just accepted my leadership and trusted me.

Passing the bridle above his ears would send him into a nervous rebellion, where I would be pinned against the walls or projected away from him. Someone had pulled his ears to punish him during previous training, and the idea of letting another human touch his ears would send him in uncontrollable panic.

One July afternoon, after thirty minutes of pure battle, I got so frustrated that I sent him back to his pasture and saddled one of the lesson horses for my upcoming session. For close to two weeks I came to the stable, ignored Storm, avoided eye contact with him, and took lessons on other horses. I remembered Jake's body language when he walked past the big brown and white Siamese cat named Blue. He walked confident and calm and did not make eye contact.

Blue seemed to be drawn to Jake and decided to accept him.

After two weeks of pure avoidance, walking with confidence past his pasture, one early morning I took Storm out of his stall and presented the bridle to him; he lowered his head in respect and let me put his bridle on without a fuss. This was the first day of our life long conversation. He was ready to listen. I decided that every new lesson I wanted to teach him, I would give him time to think about it with a calm and assertive demeanor so that he knew what I expected from him but that there was nothing to fear from me. This was the best decision I could have taken. Everyone else around him had wanted immediate results at all cost, and because of his untamed Arabian horse spirit, he had become combative. I had engaged in conversation with him, and he was listening, but he was still testing me and others.

I was late one day for a lesson; my trainer had been trying to tack up Storm to save time. Unfortunately, he wanted no part of her, and as I turned the corner to enter the main hall, there she was, holding on to the reins, facing the belly and menacing front hooves of the gray Arabian. She stood at an angle, putting her weight into the reins, as he was raring up, barely missing the ceiling wood rafters of the low-profile barn.

It was impressive, the size, the power, and fury of this beautiful beast. He was so angry and so scared at the same time. I helped her calm him down, and we canceled the lesson. I spent the next hour doing ground work with him to show him kindness and leadership and help him enjoy our time together. As time went by, I saw his eyes soften and his neck relax, and all became much easier. He enjoyed working ground exercises in the arena without his bridle. I would sing to him and do a little dance: two steps forward, two steps back, one step to the right, and one step to the left. He would follow me in rhythm, his shoulder close to mine like he was reading my mind, when in fact he understood so well my body motion that he knew what my next step would be. We were slowly becoming a duo, but my occasional mistakes would set him back, so I would have to work harder to gain his total trust.

I was still leasing him, and I had not yet taken the decision to buy him, because at the time, I was wondering if he was not too much of a horse for me. But each step of progress we made seemed to bring us closer. One day, arriving at the stable in a late morning, I noticed that Storm's pasture gate was open. He was not in his stall or in the pasture. The other horses were grazing quietly, so I closed the gate and grabbed his halter that was hanging on the fence and went looking for him.

It did not take long until I spotted him, daring and arrogant, trotting from one side of the large dressage arena to the other side. I walked up to the entrance, mesmerized by his raw beauty, his silver tail high on his rump flying in the wind, his nostrils dilated blowing air forcefully; he looked at me and took off in a majestic canter, and then a trot, throwing his head from right to left and up and down.

I watched for a while absorbing the magical scene

of his daring beauty, but it was time to open the conversation. I stepped in the arena, invading the stage of his powerful dance. I called his name in a stern voice. He turned around and faced me, pawing the ground angrily and staring right at me from the far corner of the arena. And then he took off like a wild animal toward me, sending a cloud of sand in the air behind him. I took a deep breath and focused on my breathing, planting my feet and waiting with my eyes calmly but sternly staring at him. The possibility of getting hurt was real, but I chose to stand my ground like I had seen Jake doing on so many occasions. I had to believe that Storm was trying his last attempt to intimidate me, like Blue had done several times with Jake.

Two yards away from me, Storm stopped abruptly in a cloud of sand, his whole weight shifted on his hind legs. He stood for a moment looking at me; then he lowered his head, his ears still erect toward me; he walked a few steps closer and tucked his nose into my chest. I felt inebriated by the experience. My heart was pounding with the realization that this beautiful, spirited Arabian horse had accepted me as his human. He had "joined" with me.

On that same day, I purchased Storm and came home euphoric. I was happy with the results of our hard work, about Storm's training and about our farm that was taking shape. We were blessed, but the happiness was to be short-lived, because life always presents challenges, and our world was going to be turned upside down.

One morning I noticed that Peanut was not eating.

She had not had any health problems for years, and I just thought that maybe she had a tummy ache. The evening meal was much better, but she looked like she was struggling to finish her food. I kept an eye on her for the next few days. One meal she would eat and the next she would struggle, so I decided to take her to the clinic.

The blood test did not bring any conclusive result. We got her on antibiotics just in case there was an infection, and the decision was made to feed her for a while food that she could not resist. I made chicken, omelets, and anything I thought she would eat, but Peanut was starting to lose weight, vomiting when she ate. I was desperate to find an answer. We did not know what we were looking at.

Peanut's vet started to suspect cancer, so he sent us to the oncologist at the Gulf Coast animal clinic in Houston. They are a wonderful facility, featured recently on the Nat Geo Wild channel, on a television program named *Animal ER*. Their expertise includes oncology, dermatology, dental, neurology and more. The clinic was huge, with people and pets coming and going. Peanut was by then no more than a little shadow, terribly skinny and very sad to look at. I had the feeling that everyone was looking at us and judging us for not feeding our dog, I felt horribly ashamed.

We talked to the doctor while he was looking at her, palpating various areas around her throat. Then a young man came to take her for x-rays, and we were sent back to the waiting room. After what seemed like an eternity, they brought her back to us and the doctor came to meet with us and discuss Peanut's condition. We followed him to the examination room where the x-rays were up on the light fixture.

Even though I have no medical back ground, I could tell that there were spots all over her body. My heart jumped into my throat as I struggled to hold back the tears that wanted to flow out of my eyes. Peanut's body was invaded with cancerous tumors. There was no surgery, no treatment that could help her, she was literally starving to death because the throat tumors were making her gag when she ate.

Why didn't I not notice something was wrong before she stopped eating, before it was too late? I felt so guilty, but Peanut had been playing with Xena on our land a few weeks before, and she looked perfectly healthy. Animals instinctively hide pain and weakness because in the wild, weakness makes them more vulnerable to predators. Peanut had courageously and instinctively held her composure until she could not anymore, until the cancer had taken over every ounce of her will and there was no more fight in her.

I decided on that day that I would not let her suffer any longer, and despite Allan's refusal to accept her terminal stage, and his hurtful criticism, I made an appointment for my vet to come to our home to help her die before she would starve completely. It was November 20, 1998. I took the day off from work to be with her. We spent the whole afternoon in the living room, snuggling on the sofa. I wanted her to know how much she was loved until the very second when the needle went into her front paw. I was holding her in my arms, big tears rolling silently down my cheeks. She slowly closed her eyes, falling into a peaceful sleep. The doctor asked me if I was ready. I nodded, and the lethal liquid was injected.

I remember following the flow in the short transparent tube to the needle in her vein and having a sense of panic, asking myself if I had done the right thing and having the sinking feeling that it was too late to change my mind. Peanut drifted away, taking with her a large piece of my heart.

Jake was with us the whole time, silent, staring at me. He did not move until it was all over; then he came closer and put his nose gently on Peanut's neck. I think he knew she was gone, and he felt our pain. We went to get Xena from the yard, so that she too could have closure. She walked around the room, sniffing at the air, and never came close to Peanut's body. She knew she was already gone; maybe Peanut's spirit was still in the room for a last good-bye to her best friend.

We drove all the way to our land to bury Peanut, where I had dreamed to bring Xena, Jake, and her to romp and play and live happily ever after. When the grave was covered, and the night was all around us, the weight of my pain ravaged through my soul, and I could hardly walk back to the truck. My legs were giving out under me. I felt drained, and Allan had to help me sit in the truck and breathe through the sobbing that was shaking my whole body.

I cried so much when she was gone. I felt so alone and guilty in the decision process that for three days after we buried her, I could not bring myself to eat, get out of bed, or even wash. Allan tried to cheer me up, but I was inconsolable; nothing could bring me out of my sadness, except Jake, who would put his big nose on the bed and stare at me without moving for hours, and I realized that he was not going to give up on me until I got up and kept moving, so I did.

Xena, for a few days, moped around the house, looking for her playmate, so Jake let her have his favorite toy, the soccer ball. From that day on, she carried the ball everywhere she went and would deposit it by my feet for me to throw. She would repeat ten to twenty times the process, until I would get tired and send her away. It was like she needed a substitute for the fun she had with Peanut, and the soccer ball had become her best friend.

Xena with Jake's soccer ball.

A Wise Dog Named Jake

Grief is a natural response to any important loss, and in the case of losing someone, mourning inspires compassion from everyone, but when someone loses a pet, a part of society stays insensitive to the grieving a pet owner goes through.

After only three days of mourning Peanut, going to work with swelling eyes only amplified the struggle I was faced with. I did not tell my co-workers or my boss of my loss, only a couple of friends whom I knew would be empathetic; so I withdrew into a quiet stage, struggling to just concentrate on work and trying my best to refrain from crying. I would come home exhausted and relieved to finally be able to grieve without holding back.

Grief is the emotional reaction when a person loses a loved one. It is also the process of adjusting to life after the loss, releasing the pain in order to move forward in a healthy way. Grieving is a personal battle. Depending on your loss and who you are, your process of grieving will be different from another person's experience.

Mourning for me always meant to find a goal and accomplish it to reach an emotional and rational closure. The stable and apartment were slowly taking shape, but there was still a lot to do before we could move in or sell our home. The void that Peanut's absence had carved into my heart pulled at my very soul, and I wanted to be by her side, on our land as soon as possible, so we worked harder, and we put the house up for sale the end of January 1999, before the apartment was ready to move in. To our surprise, within a few days of being on the market, our house had four offers by potential buyers. The apartment was not near livable yet, but we accepted an offer and started the process. We had thirty days to finish construction on our farm, pack, store some of our furniture, and move the rest we would use into the tiny apartment.

In March of 1999, on a stormy day, we left our house of over ten years and moved into a small apartment half its size, in our barely finished horse stable. Storm came to live with us as soon as the fences were up, and even though there was a hole in my heart, I was happy to finally be on our land, and be closer not only to Storm, Jake, and Xena but also to Peanut and her peaceful resting place.

Our beautiful red barn.

Chapter 8

Life on the Farm

Having lived in a Houston neighborhood where stray dogs are a common occurrence, I always drove with dog food and water in my car, as well as a leash. My promise to Coal to always look out for any stranded animal was still alive. One summer day, I was driving down a busy road when I noticed an old black dog standing on the middle shoulder, looking at the cars passing by. He was panting, and I was worried that he was lost. I stopped by the Lillie's, a beautiful property with rows of oak trees along the majestic driveway. I ran across the street to reach the dog.

He was friendly, but looked stressed by the summer heat, so I decided to invite him into my air-conditioned Ford Explorer. I am a 120-pound. woman; this old boy must have weighed 80 pounds. I knew immediately by the way he looked at me when I opened the rear door that he was not going to make the effort to jump in. So I put my arms around his large chest underneath his front legs, and I gave him a good lift. I succeeded putting his stretched-out paws on top of the back-cargo carpet. He stood there on two legs, wagging his tail, quite satisfied with himself, but still with no intention to jump in. I gathered my strength, grabbed his rump, and lifted him up, pushing him inside with all I had.

A Wise Dog Named Jake

He stood facing the AC vent, his tongue dripping over the back seat, content to feel the cool breeze on his muzzle. We set out to the neighborhood across the street to find his home. We stopped at every yard where someone was outside working to ask if they knew whom the old dog belonged to. I had started losing hope, when one of my inquiries was answered positively. "He belongs to the Lillie's" said the man with a smile. I must have had a funny expression on my face, because the man repeated that he was sure the dog belonged to the people at the Lillie's. I was relieved and embarrassed at the same time. I had picked the dog up just across from the Lillie's, near the neighborhood where I was standing. I thanked the man and headed across the street to enter the beautiful shaded driveway that led to the house. The old dog was wagging his tail and smiling at me when I opened the back door to let him out. I turned around, a little red in the face, and went on my merry way.

Living close to the countryside was different from that in the cities. People would regularly let their dogs roam free, and I had to be careful not to "rescue" neighbors' dogs.

Life at the farm was fun. I had bought another horse, a beautiful Arabian named Rhapsody Blue, who had one blue and one brown eye. Storm and Rhapsody rapidly became inseparable pasture mates. I paid very little for Rhapsody, a registered Egyptian Arabian gelding, because he had not been handled or ridden for years. I had to make sure Allan, a novice rider, would not be in danger.

I started with ground work in our arena. Horses are

flight animals; if they are uncomfortable with a situation, they will run. So I let him run, giving him pointers when to turn and change direction so that he would keep his focus on me and not on the flight. At some point, he lowered his head, keeping one ear pointed in my direction, he started licking his lips, a clear indication that he wanted to listen to me. I had opened the discussion, and when I put the saddle on his back, it took only a few bucks before he accepted it. I asked him to stand, and I let him rest while I rubbed his face, neck, and flank with the reins to show him that there was nothing to fear. When his eyes went soft and his breathing was slow, I eased myself onto his back, and we went for a slow walk and a lovely trot followed with a magnificent canter. Rhapsody had not only conquered Storm's respect and friendship but also won my admiration with his smooth and perfect gaits and beautiful conformation.

A few weeks later came a third horse, owned by a nearby resident, to complete and fill our three-stall barn. She was a large quarter horse mare and I was initially concerned that rivalry would set in between Storm and Rhapsody, but it never did. Storm was always respectful with mares and inspired leadership in geldings, so I was not surprised to see the new mare totally comfortable with Storm's friendly assertiveness and Rhapsody's quiet acceptance. The geldings would groom each other's crest and mane for extended periods, while standing in the shade of the large trees bordering the pasture. The mare, oblivious, would be grazing quietly by the nearby tree, when Storm would approach her and somehow convince her that it was time for the same bonding ritual, and they would stand shoulder to shoulder, closing their eyes as they ran their muzzles onto each other's thick manes.

When it was time to feed, Storm took ownership of his stall first, while the other two competed for the next stalls. If a scuffle erupted, Storm would pin his ears back and stretch his beautiful long Arabian neck toward the mare and the gelding, and somehow, they would hurry and settle in their respective stalls. I would watch for the opportune time to close their doors so that I could pour the grain into each bucket, and then I would stand by Storm's shoulder while he ate quietly, allowing me to groom and love on him. This was our time to bond and just be in each other's life. Near him, I was fully in tune with his powerful but gentle personality, and when I would put my head against his neck and feel the softness of his thick mane on my face, his scent would calm my soul despite the kind of day I had. At times he would bend his neck around my shoulders like an embrace, and I would hold out my hand and press his cheek against mine, closing my eyes to fully appreciate the delight in my heart.

On the other side of the fence, Xena, for her part, was obsessed with Jake's soccer ball, and every day after work I had to throw the ball repeatedly until my arm hurt. She was young, full of energy, and had lost her running partner when Peanut had died, so our game was very important to her.

Jake would quietly watch us from the small patio we had built for him by the doggy door. He would spend hours basking in the spring sun. After playing with Xena, I would sit next to him and just listen to the birds, stroking his head gently and talking to him softly. I could tell his eyes where not as bright and his gait was a little wobbly, but he still knew how to inspire respect, even from Xena who was at times a little rambunctious. His muzzle was all white and his back was stiff. It pained him to get up and step over the doggy door despite the pain medication, but his appetite was still good, and he enjoyed our everyday talk while sitting outside watching the birds and squirrels go by. I knew one day I would have to say good-bye to my faithful companion, my guardian, my teacher, my friend. But for now, I wanted to cherish the moments we had together and feel the breeze caressing our skin and enjoy together the peace around us. "You are such a good dog Jake," I would say to him, as he looked at me with eyes filled with the unconditional love that only a dog can give.

With Peanut's death, I had lost not only my sweet shadow but also my partner in volunteering. Xena had grown out of her puppyhood, so I took her to temperament testing at Caring Critters workshop to become a therapy dog. She was instantly a hit and passed the test like a pro. The residents loved her because she would meticulously go from one wheelchair to the next, without much coaching from me, making sure she did not miss anyone. She was gentle with the frail ladies and playful with the younger residents. She was a natural, so I continued volunteering with her, and we brought sunshine where there was so much sadness. I had noticed that the elderlies' blank faces would suddenly awaken, their faraway stares would instantly focus and shine, and the slumped silhouettes would sit up and wave at us when we walked into the facilities with the dogs. The residents would smile, pointing at the dogs with trembling hands. Xena would remind them of a dog they knew when they were children, or they would be curious how I had taught her to do all the tricks she did to entertain them, and they would smile and laugh with us. Through the joy we were bringing to them, I saw my dad's face many times. I was paying forward what he had done for me and others during the tormented life he had courageously lived until the end.

One Monday late afternoon, after dinner, I watched Jake take a step toward the doggy door; he was uncertain, he turned his head, looked at me, and collapsed, eyes wide open, staring at the empty space above him. I rushed to him and held him in my arms, tears rolling down my cheeks, I thought it was the end, but Jake looked at me, and his tail thumped the floor softly. "I love you Jake," I told him, still holding onto him. Allan came into the room alarmed, and we brought Jake to his bed where we stayed the entire night. We hugged him, talked to him, and reminisced about all the experiences we had lived together, the travels and adventures, the joys and the pains, and the fears and the prides. We had been blessed to have been a part of his life and to have had him to protect us, and now we wanted to protect him and assure him that we would stay with him until the end. Jake closed his eyes forever the next morning, it was July 20, 1999. We buried him next to Peanut, under a large tree, in the pasture behind the stable.

Jake came into our lives shortly after Allan and I moved in together. He was with us through every event of our life as a couple, always watching after me and protecting me when I was alone. He taught me to observe body language to understand animals and people. I learned by watching him that being calm and how you project yourself is half of the battle. The other half is made up of tolerance, respect, and persistence. Losing him was like losing an old teacher, a best friend, and a part of myself.

After Jake died, Xena and I spent more time playing and volunteering, but I knew she was lonely most of the time. When I got home every day, after retrieving the ball several times, she would watch me saddle Storm. I would take her with me when I rode in the ranch prairies at the end of my street. She would trot ahead of the horse, making sure she always stayed out of reach of his hooves, always keeping an eye for any change in direction. I would give Storm a little leg to ask him to trot or canter; Xena would keep up the pace, despite the rough terrain. Back at the farm, if I was not paying attention, she would run the horses back into their stalls.

Storm and Xena had a love-hate relationship. He did not like to be herded, but he would entice her to run, prancing in front of her, tail up and rolling his head side to side and up and down, and the race around the pasture would start. Neither of them would give in, until I would step in and interrupt them for fear that one of them would get hurt. It was obvious to me that Xena needed a smaller friend than Storm; she needed a dog companion. My heart was not healed from losing Jake or even Peanut. It was difficult to even think of accepting another dog into my broken heart. I could not bring myself to go to a shelter to find a dog. I knew somehow a dog would find me when it was time.

A friend of mine had rescued a young pregnant dog, and a few weeks after Jake died, she called me, anxious because she had several puppies and needed help to place them in good homes. I accepted the challenge, and as soon as the puppies were weaned, we placed all but two in permanent homes. Allan and I discussed the possibility of adopting one of the puppies, so I told my friend we would look at them.

She brought both dogs to meet Xena and see if the chemistry between them would help us choose. Both puppies were adorable balls of fur, with big paws and beautiful heads. The mother was a red colored shepherd mix, but it was very apparent that the father must have been a Rottweiler. Xena did not show much interest in the puppies at first, so I decided to examine them. The little brindle colored one was very playful; the fuzz on her back was so soft she felt like a stuffed animal. The second puppy was more quiet, inquisitive, and explored alone in the stable. She walked with a purpose. She was tri-color with a black back, a white chest, and the brown markings of the Rottweiler with adorable eye brows.

I called to her, and she came trotting toward me, her oversized paws tapping the ground in excitement. I grabbed her little face to look right into her eyes, and I was taken aback. "She has Jake's eyes," I heard myself say softly, as I stroke her head and rubbed her body. "I'll take this one," I told my friend, pointing a finger at the tri-color puppy. When everyone had left, I picked her up and stared at her eyes one more time. It was not only the shape of her eyes or their color that reminded me of Jake, it was also the shine and spark that animated them. I decided to call her Cheyenne, because it was a strong name, from a proud people, and it seemed to fit her personality. The next day, I still had that strange feeling about Cheyenne's eyes, when I called my friend to inquire about the date the puppies were born.

"They were born on July 20," I heard her say, and my heart jumped in my throat, because I realized that Cheyenne was born the day Jake died.

Cheyenne sleeping under her mom's paw in the front.

Xena loving on baby Cheyenne.

Cheyenne, Xena, and I, the inseparable trio.

Epilogue

Many years have passed, Jake, since you walked beside me. I have never forgotten the lessons you taught me. Because of you I remain calm in the face of adversity, and I never give up on the things or the people or the animals I believe in.

Writing this book has been a journey back to our time together. It has been fun and sad at the same time, but it brought me closer to you, despite the years that have gone by. I am very thankful for each time you put yourself in danger to protect me. I still remember the terrified face of the young man who was following me in the dark, when you stood in front of him, all teeth out. You looked so dangerous, he believed everything you told him.

I sit outside often, feeling the breeze on my face, listening to the birds, and watching the squirrels running on the highway in the trees, like we used to do. Cheyenne, the puppy born the day of your passing, has surpassed all my expectations. She not only has your eyes, but she is also wise, kind, and respectful as you were, but somehow, I think you know that.

So much has changed since you left; the farm house is built with a large wraparound porch, like I always wanted. Xena disappeared on New Year's Eve 2000. We think the fireworks frightened her, she ran away and got lost, but you and I know that Xena knew well the area and would not have been turned around. I think that someone got to her. I looked for her for six months. It was a really dark time for me; my heart was hurting, but I could not give up on her. Every minute that I was not at work was consumed with the goal of finding her, making and distributing flyers, calling anyone who could help, or visiting shelters. The *Houston Chronicle* ran a story about her and her work at the elderly home. The article on the front page displayed the last picture I had taken of Xena, during a Halloween visit. On top of the picture in bold letters it read: "Retirement Center Residents Missing Therapy Dog." It went on saying, that even though many animals are visiting the elderly home within the scope of Caring Critters, Xena was an obvious favorite. "I was always thrilled to see Xena," said resident Sheila B. "I knew Xena well. She was one of my favorites," said Phil D. another resident, "she was quite a pup, I think she was a good influence on some of the people here," Phil said. In fact, Xena was so interactive that everyone wanted to pet her, wherever we went.

During my quest to find her, I was able to reach local television channels. Two of them ran a fifteen-minute story on the six o-clock news. The day after she went missing, despite a bad bronchitis that was pulling me down, I stood an entire day outside our neighborhood in the cold, with a life-size picture of Xena glued to a cardboard. A young mother and her daughter stopped by to give me hot chocolate and wish me luck. Her kind gesture gave me the strength to stay a little longer. I gave out thousands of flyers during the months that followed, and even though I received many phone calls, none of the sightings got me closer to finding her. The staff at the retirement home where we volunteered posted a sign on the marquee, pleading for her safe return: "Help us find Xena". They took the sandwich sign I had made on the first day and took turns wearing it along the freeway. It was heartwarming to see the outpouring of compassion and love. The unwanted puppy who had found her way to my house, the fifty-two-pound Rottweiler mix who had won our hearts and the hearts of the residents, had touched so many lives, that all of us were praying for her return.

Allan left us a few months after she disappeared. I guess he thought I was obsessed with finding her, and it was a "bad thing." He had his own demons and had to find his happiness elsewhere, so Cheyenne stood with me, alone, like you did so many times before. You would be proud of her; she protected me, hunted for me, volunteered with me, and was there when I cried and when I laughed.

I wanted to write this book, not only to honor you, Jake, but also to promote stray dogs' adoptions. So many wonderful four-legged animals are dumped every day in the streets or county roads to fend for themselves. Despite the sad or even ugly physical shape they might be in when they timidly approach passers-by, they can grow into beautiful, smart, and giving members of families. I am so glad you found us, Jake, when you were hungry, and I am thankful to Allan for inviting you in.

About the Author

Brigitte Finkiewicz started writing poetry at an early age as presents to her mother and father. When she was eight years old, she wrote two short stories involving animal heroes. She stopped writing soon after her father died; she felt as if her muse had died with him.

Brigitte worked in the oil business for over thirty-three years. She retired in 2016 after spending nearly twenty-eight years with the same company.

She continues to volunteer her time with Caring Critters, visiting a retirement home with her rescued German Shepherd.

She is still actively helping horses and dogs when need arises and manages a small B and B, welcoming travelers into the stable apartment where she had lived with Jake.

She still resides at the farm with her partner David.

Made in the USA
Coppell, TX
22 February 2022

73955243R00079